i

Fourteenth Edition

A CHANGING CALIFORNIA

Jack Carney

CONSENSUS PUBLISHERS

ii

Editor: John A. Bradley

A CHANGING CALIFORNIA. Fourteenth Edition

2009 Jack Carney. All Rights Reserved

Printed in the United States of America
For information address Consensus Publishers,

9869 Karmont Avenue, South Gate, CA 90280

For inquiries or orders, please fax: (562) 806-2633

ISBN 1-879861-28-3

iii

To
My eldest brother, James Kearney,
born 1907, Oklahoma Indian Territory

To
Natalya Alcerro

To
Angela Alcerro

To
Catherine Maeve Sheehan

To
Rossy Eguigure

To
Martha (Welch) Carney

To
Deborah Campbell

To
Manuel Servín

and to
Eve and Jack Carney Monaghan

TABLE OF CONTENTS—AND PRINCIPAL TOPICS

Preface

Having completed the writing of this fourteenth edition of *A Changing California,* I again renew my original hopes for my efforts--that my work helps readers gain a considerably more substantial understanding of the governance of the most change-oriented community in the world, how it came into being, and how it is changing. Like its earlier versions this fourteenth edition is particularly a brief but comprehensive description of the important prevailing circumstances, problems, structures, and functions of California politics and government.

Happily, with the sometimes arduous task of bringing a new edition of a book into existence comes the felicitous opportunity to thank those who inspired or assisted. I specially thank here Joe Dana, founder and first President of Consensus Publishers, Inc., John A. Bradley, who edited my entire manuscript, and all who reviewed my work. Particular thanks to Professor Mike Kennedy, Professor Bill Loiterman, David Berger, M.D., Angela Alcerro, and Mark Day. And for those who in other ways encouraged my efforts I am grateful: Angela Ianni, Bruce Unruh, Jack Murphy, Edgar F. Love, Jim O'Grady, Seán E. Carney and Kim Carney, Nancy Muñoz, reference librarian, Downey City Library, and Mario and Crystal de Leon.

I also acknowledge my debt to all from whose research and writing I have drawn, but any error of fact or opinion is my own.

Jack Carney

INTRODUCTORY CHAPTER:

A CHANGED AND CHANGING CALIFORNIA

SECTOR I: AMERICAN CONQUEST OF CALIFORNIA

ALWAYS AN ANGLOPHONE EMPIRE*

American imperialism began in the early years of the American colonies when Anglo colonists, using modern European weapons, descended upon the American Indian tribes and their lands.** Virginia fought five wars with the American Indians before 1760. The Puritans fought six.

But our first major war, the American Revolution (1775-1783) was against imperialism (British). Not surprisingly, only about one third of the American people supported the revolution. The numerically dominant Anglo-Americans (inhabitants of the U.S. of English origin or descent) almost completely sat out the war here, or moved to Canada.***

The war over, the numerically dominant Anglo-Americans and allies framed basic documents designed to build an American empire.**** The Articles of Confederation (1776) purposely did not fix western borders. And Thomas Jefferson (author of the Declaration of Independence) writing to James Madison (father of the Constitution), celebrated the fact that " ... no constitution was ever before so well designed as ours (U.S. constitution) for extending extensive empire." ****

---

*An Anglophone empire is an English-speaking empire. The International Encyclopedia of the Social Sciences defines imperialism as"...the exercise of any form of political control or influence by one community over another."

** Other Europeans did similarly in most of the rest of the Western Hemisphere.

***There were probably more Irish than Anglo-Americans in George Washington's army, more Kellys than Smiths. This, even though Anglo-Americans outnumbered Irish in the American population by a 16-1 margin. See Committee on Linguistics and National Stocks in the U.S., *Summary of National Stocks in 1790 America.* (Washington, D.C., U.S. Government Printing Office, 1932).

****George Washington described America as a "nascent empire."

PATHS TO THE CONQUEST OF CALIFORNIA

In 1804, President Thomas Jefferson launched our first manor imperialist venture — the Louisiana Purchase. Napoleon sold the area for about $15 million, about three cents an acre.* The Purchase included the area from the Mississippi River to the Rocky Mountains. Jefferson called this new territory "an empire for liberty." It was not. It meant extension of black slavery, put the lives and property of American Indians in jeopardy, exposed Californians to attack, and increased the possibility of slavery in California. On the eve of leaving office, Jefferson asserted that" ...we must have Florida and Cuba."

In 1812, President James Madison sought to seize Canada, the greatest real estate grab in the history of the world. But the U.S. Army performed miserably. This caused the dominant Anglo-American Army officer corps to plan to repair its tainted image by attacking Mexico and taking at least the Province of California. But California was saved for a number of years by differences in the U.S. over the extension of slavery. Later, Madison ordered the annexation of West Florida.

Before the U.S.-Mexican War began in 1846, President James Polk warned the European powers from interfering with the war (in which the U.S. was clearly an aggressor). This statement was a reversal of the Monroe Doctrine of 1823, which before this was a defensive statement. Polk used it as an imperialist weapon. Polk, Jefferson, and Madison were all imperialists.

THE CONQUEST OF CALIFORNIA

Before 1848, several presidents sought to buy Mexico's Province of California. Mexico refused to sell. In 1846, President James Polk, who himself tried to buy California, decided on war to force Mexico to sell.

Among those opposing the U.S.-Mexican War over California was Abraham Lincoln (later president). Lincoln held that what he called the "dirty little war" was unconstitutional. The U.S. House agreed. Lincoln also introduced "spot resolutions" into the U.S. House challenging Polk to name the spot where he claimed Mexico " ... shed American blood on American soil." Polk could not name the spot because there was no such spot.**

---

*Why did Napoleon sell? First, there were the carrots (the $15 million). Second, there was the stick, a veiled threat that the U.S. would take the area if he would not sell. We knew that he could not defend the area. The British Navy, wishing to bottle him up in Europe, would not let him resupply or reinforce.

**When President Polk attacked and conquered California in 1846-1848, he was seeking to extend slavery. But he said that he was extending democracy, a ruse used by many empires to mask their true intentions. He also presented the U.S. as a holy Joseph. No empire is a holy Joseph. Empire's goals are always the same, perceived advantages for themselves.

John Quincy Adams (former president) also opposed the war, as did Ulysses S. Grant (future president). General Grant, who fought in the war, said it was "... one of the most unjust wars ever waged by a stronger against a weaker power."

Regardless of political opposition, in 1846, Polk sent a force under General Stephen Watts Kearny into thinly populated California. Governor Pío Pico mounted a fierce resistance.

In December, Don Pío's brother, Andrés, leading a civilian force of Californians, intercepted the invading U.S. Army Dragoons at San Pascual, northeast of San Diego, and inflicted a crushing defeat. But after San Pascual, outnumbered and vastly outgunned, California resistance weakened and collapsed..

PÍO PICO. Last Governor of the Province of California before the U.S. occupation, pictured with his wife, MARÍA YGNACIA ALVARADO PICO.

The Pico family was founded by the Pico brothers' mestizo grandfather and mulata grandmother, who also helped found the city of San Francisco on July 4, 1776.

After losing in California, Mexico still refused to sell the Province of California. President Polk then decided on an expanded war on Mexico's center of power in southern Mexico.

There were four major battles in the war — all of them south of California. The U.S. won all four. Mexico lacked sufficient artillery and ammunition.

Tragically, the seizing and holding of California for the U.S. meant that an estimated 40,000 Mexicans were to die. * Lamentably, U.S. deaths exceeded 13,000. Most of the American dead were poor, and risked their lives for $7.00 per month.

---

* Estimate by Abiel Livermore, *The War with Mexico Revisited.* (Boston: American Peace Society, 1850).

THE "SALE"

The war over, the U.S. pushed the "sale" of the Province of California, which was about half of Mexico. It was sold for $15 million, about six cents an acre.

Mexico feared that if it did not capitulate to the "sale," the U.S. would take still more of Mexico. But the U.S. did not want to take very populous southern Mexico in 1848. It did not want to risk a long guerilla war there, and did not want millions of Mexicans voting in American elections. Finally, the U.S. Senate, satisfying a voracious popular appetite for land, approved the Mexican Cession by a vote of 38-14. Again, politics trumped principle.

Frederick Douglass, the leading black intellectual of the 19th century, said that the U.S."... robbed Mexico of the most important and most valuable of her territory..." *
Robert Kennedy said that the U.S.-Mexican War was "...a dark page in American history."

Douglass

The American State of California was by far the most important part of the Mexican Cession. The Cession also included the present States of Nevada and Utah, most of Arizona and New Mexico, and parts of Colorado, Texas and Wyoming. The taking of California positioned the U.S. eventually to command the seas, which itself is an empire.

*Frederick Douglass, Editorial in the *Rochester North Star*, March 17, 1848.

U.S. ARMY TORTURES AND HANGINGS — AND THE COVER-UP

The dominant Anglo-American U.S. Army officer corps was, during the U.S.-Mexican War, torturing their soldiers and prisoners with rawhide beatings, beatings with officers' swords and brandings with cattle branding irons.* It was in this climate that over 5,300 regular army soldiers who saw duty in the war deserted. Over 700 Irish soldiers deserted, and following their conscience. formed a separate Irish Battalion (known as the *Patricios*), changed sides (to Mexico) and defended Mexico's Province of California, the real U.S. target. A number of Mexicans and Germans, several Scots and English, and a sprinkling of men from other nations joined them. The *Patricios* fought in the front lines in the four major battles of the war. **

The Irish liked Mexicans and Mexican culture. They hated Anglo-Americans. This was not only because of the beatings and brandings, but also because of the British-Anglo imperialists' attempts to exterminate them in Ireland, and for British-Anglo attitudes, for instance, the editorial in the *London Times* expressing the hope that with the potato famine in Ireland (mid and late 1840s) that "... the native Irishman would be as rare on the banks of the Liffy (Dublin) as the red man is on the banks of the Manhattan (New York)." *** Little wonder that the most generous entity helping victims of the famine were the Choctaw Indians.

In the final battle of the war (at Churubusco) 62 percent of the Irish Battalion were killed. Eighty-five were captured when they ran out of ammunition. Forty-nine of these were immediately sentenced to be hanged by military court-martial. The *Patricios* had no legal counsel, no appeal, and no federal court review. They were not permitted to introduce information about imperialism, racial, ethnic, or religious discrimination, or the beatings or brandings.

The U.S. Army selected William Harney, a notorious sadist. as hangman. Notably, he honed his hanging skills on Indians in the Seminole and Blackhawk Wars, and was indicted in St. Louis for beating a black woman to death. For the latter, the army transferred him to avoid trial. (He was never tried.). He was then promoted to Colonel. At the hangings of the *Patricios*, he engaged in many violations of the 8th Amendment (which forbids cruel or unusual punishment) and the Articles of War. After the hangings, Colonel Harney was promoted to brigadier general.

One of those hanged (Francis O'Connor) had lost both legs at Churubusco. Harney ordered him brought from the hospital unconscious and hanged.

---

*The U.S. (in 1861) banned the army's use of rawhide beatings. In the Civil War both Generals Grant and Lee discouraged brandings (banned in 1871).

**Many soldiers changed sides in the American Revolution. They were seldom punished.

*** See Seumas McManus, *Story of the Irish Race.* New York: Konecky and Konecky and the Devin-Adair Company, 1921, p. 610.

THE COVER-UP

The U.S. Army for many years successfully covered up its records of torturers and hangings in 1846-1848. But in 1917, Congressmen Coleman and Greene got Congress to force the U.S. Army to put its records of 1846-1848 in the National Archives – albeit without notice. It was not until the late 1990s with Mark Day's documentary and a spate of well-researched books using Irish, Mexican, and U.S. Archives, and contemporary nongovernmental sources that the full and accurate account became available to the world.*

CONQUEST OF THE CALIFORNIA INDIANS

Indians, of course, discovered California. The California Indians, here for perhaps 15,000 years, lived under Spanish law (1769-1822) and loose Mexican rule (1822-1846). They constituted the bulk of California's population (about 150,000) at the beginning of the U.S. - Mexican War (1846).

But under American military rule (1846-1849) and early California state rule (beginning in 1849) their number was vastly reduced. This was not only because of disease, but by reason of being subjected to onerous abuses.

During the early years of California rule, our first governor under statehood, Peter Burnett (1849-1851), famously stated that "... a war of extermination will continue to be waged between the races until the Indians become extinct." The first California Legislature paid settler militias $1.1 million to hunt down Indians.

By 1860, about 10 years after statehood, the Indian population plunged from about 150,000 to about 30,000. U.C.L.A. historian John Caughey described this as "heartless liquidation."**

But today, due to the generosity of California voters, we gave the California Indians a virtual monopoly of casino gambling by passing Proposition 1-A. They rescued them from being completely powerless politically. With less than 1/2 of 1 percent of California's population, by the early 2000s, they became the most powerful lobby in California, and the biggest contributors to political campaigns. Though not responsible for the crimes of their forebears, the voters have taken giant steps to remedy historic wrongdoings.

Lamentably, the best intentions of the voters have been partially defeated by the fact that only about 10 percent of California Indians profit directly from tribal-owned casinos. Also, casino-owning tribes have successfully pressured government to block poor Indian tribes' attempts to open their own casinos. Some large casino-owning tribes virulently oppose unionization of their workers.

In 2008, California voters approved expansion of Indian casinos. California will gain a bit economically. On the other hand, are there not some bad effects on California's society? In a word, it is. It will create gambling addicts, more divorces, job losses, and stealing. Professor William Thompson of the University of Nevada found that gambling addicts commit suicide more than any other type of addict. Finally, gambling addiction especially devastate the lives of children.

---

*See Mark Day, *The San Patricios, A Video Recording* (Vista, CA: San Patricio Productions. 1996).

**John W. Caughey, *California* (Englewood Cliffs. N. J. Prentice-Hall, Inc., 1953) p. 339.

A RECONQUISTA?

Chicano activists remind that the Southwest is Mexican *irredenta* (Mexican land taken forcibly by the U.S.),* reject the validity of the U.S. — Mexico border, and hold that the issue of undocumented migration across it by Mexican nationals should be moot.

Clearly, the U.S. will not voluntarily return the Province of California to Mexico. And as the dominant power it will continue to enforce the border as legal. It is the law of the jungle today, just as it was in 1848.

But do not Mexican "illegals" recently migrating to the Province of California think that they are part of *a reconquista?*** No, they do not. Nor do they wish a reattachment of the Province to Mexico. They do not forget why they left Mexico. Nevertheless, most tend to feel that in the Southwest U.S. they are on their own turf.

SEGMENT II

THE BROWNING OF CALIFORNIA--AND THE REACTION

LOW BIRTH RATES OF NON-LATINO WHITES

The birth rates of non-Latino whites in the U.S. have in recent years been about 1.6 (The population replacement rate is 2.1.). At the same time, foreign born Latinas' birth rates have been about 3.7. Largely because of this disparity in birth rates, the U.S. Census Bureau predicts that well within this decade Latinos will outnumber non-Latino whites in California. The Public Policy Institute found that by 2040, non-Latino whites will be only one-third of the adult population of California.

HOW MANY LATINO RESIDENTS IN CALIFORNIA AND THE U.S. ?

There are 13.2 million Latino residents in California and 46 million in the U.S. This Latino population is propelled more by births than by all forms of immigration. Undocumented (mostly) and legal immigration of Latinos merely speed up the process of browning.* **

---

*In 1916, Francisco (Poncho) Villa attacked Columbus, New Mexico. Sixteen Americans lost their lives. Villa wanted Mexican President Carranza to make war on the U.S. to win back much of the Mexican Cession. Carranza refused.

Then, in 1917, the German foreign secretary contacted the German minister in Mexico, telling him to strive for a German-Mexican alliance. In the so-called Zimmerman Note, he promised to secure the return of a large portion of the Mexican Cession to Mexico if Mexico joined Germany in World War I. Carranza, though he took many anti-American actions, chose again not to make war against the U.S.

**In all of their marches and demonstrations, the undocumented Mexicans have proclaimed their wish to become American citizens, not to make a *reconquista.*

***Non-Latino whites will become a minority in the entire U.S. in fewer than 40 years. See Philip Martin and James Widgren, *International Migration: A Global Challenge. Population Bulletin* 51, 1, Washington, D.C.: Population Reference Bureau. 1996.

A BEAUTIFUL, EXCEEDINGLY TALENTED, AND NICE EIGHT YEAR OLD LATINA

A VIVACIOUS, BEAUTIFUL, INDUSTRIOUS, AND WONDERFUL YOUNG LATINA

MORE BROWNING BECAUSE OF THE MASSIVE RETURN OF THE NATIVE

9

Nearly three million Latino undocumented have crossed the U.S.-Mexico border and are in California, more than in any other state. Most are Indians or Mestizos from Mexico*, but many are from Central and South America.** And they are not likely to leave. No previous generation did.

THE LONG AND VARIED HISTORY
OF UNDOCUMENTED ENTRY IN AMERICA

Undocumented entry has a long and varied history in this part of the world, dating from European uninvited entry in the 1600s. Later, in the several decades before the end of the Civil War, thousands of American black slaves entered Mexico without documents to escape slavery. Today, many black Mexicans, descendants of black slaves from Spain and the U.S., live in the Mexican states of Oaxaca, Guerrero, and Veracruz.

In the early 1830s, many undocumented Americans entered the Mexican Province of Texas. In the 19th and early 20th centuries many of our ancestors from Europe entered without documents. They were not deported. Like now, we needed labor. From 1812 to 1898, many thousands of U.S. military entered Western Hemisphere nations without visas.

During World War I, and World War II, a number of Mexicans entered without documents. We needed labor. Until quite recently, we did not particularly oppose Latino undocumented border crossers.

Today, there are numbers of undocumented Canadians in New England, and Irish in New York City. Now, most undocumented are not Latino border crossers, but are visa overstayers. There are other examples.

But why do we single out Latino undocumented border crossers for nearly all enforcement, and why now? (See p. 11)

WHY HAVE UNDOCUMENTED LATINO BORDER CROSSERS BEEN ENTERING THE U.S.?

They have been coming because there is a great shortage of young workers in our aged American population.

There is also the burgeoning population of Mexico. In 1950, Mexico had about 1/5 the population of the U.S. Today, it is about 1/3. There is also great poverty in Mexico and Central America. Average workers in Mexico are paid only 22% of the wages of average American workers. In Guatemala, El Salvador, Nicaragua, and Honduras that figure is less than 10% (6 % in Honduras).

The creation of the modern undocumented Latino's is largely the result of U.S. employment and immigration practices. Decades before World War II, the U.S. welcomed millions of Mexican workers. Then there was the Mexican *Bracero* programs during and after World War II (1942-1963). These labor practices established paths to employment. Next, making things worse, federal law placed a discriminatory quota of 20,000 a year on Mexican immigration.

---

*Eighty-three percent of undocumented border crossers are Mexicans.
**There are an estimated 12 million undocumented Latinos in the U.S.

There are still other reasons. For fifty years and more, our elected political leaders on the federal level have bowed to the interests of U.S. based agricultural employers, restaurateurs, building contractors, motel and hotel owners, sweatshop owners, industrial employers, etc., all of whom engage undocumented aliens because they wish to enjoy a supply of cheap and hard-working foreign labor. And federal politicians, at taxpayers expense, pay agricultural employers huge subsidies (now over $20 billion).

With cheap labor and immense subsidies American agriculturalists can (and do) undercut Mexican subsistence farmers, thus destroying their livelihoods and the jobs of Mexican farm workers. Together there are about 2.8 million in these straits. Many will migrate to California and other American states.

Finally, there is much unemployment in Mexico since the lay-offs at *Maquiladora* factories at the border (created by the North American Free Trade Agreement). The lay-offs were caused by inability to compete with even lower wages in China.

WHY DO UNDOCUMENTED LATINO BORDER CROSSERS NOT ENTER WITH DOCUMENTS ?

Undocumented border crossing Latinos would prefer to enter the U.S. with documents (including a green work card) rather than risking their lives in an increasingly difficult crossing (over 5,000 deaths in 2008), perhaps having to pay a large sum of money to a coyote (smuggler) to aid their passage, and perhaps be apprehended.

It is often suggested that undocumented Latinos get in line behind waiting visa applicants. But the cost of applying for a visa and a green card are simply prohibitive for poor Latinos (and other poor). Making things worse, an underfunded and lethargic bureaucracy often keeps applicants waiting at the U.S.-Mexican border for weeks in hotels or in motels. (a real hardship for many). Plus, those applying for a green card are kept waiting, sometimes for years. Finally, U.S. law provides that "in most cases a relative or an employer sponsors the individual by filing an application with the U.S. Citizenship and Immigration Services." Besides there are practically no visas for agricultural workers.

THE NATIVIST ENFORCEMENT--ONLY PLAN *

Nativists (mostly Republicans) seek to secure the U.S.-Mexican border and remove as many Latino undocumented as possible with their enforcement-only design. Their plan would do the following: (1) greatly increase the Border Patrol and militarize the border, (2) erect a 700 mile fence on the border, (3) impose substantial penalties on employers hiring undocumented Latinos, and (4) oppose guest worker programs with a path to citizenship, and any other paths to citizenship. They insist that border security come before other reforms.

---

*In his classic book, *Strangers in the Land,* John Higham described Nativism as "... intense opposition to an internal minority on the ground of foreign connection."

NATIVISTS' CHIEF CHARGES AGAINST UNDOCUMENTED BORDER CROSSERS*

Nativists hold, and it is commonly thought, that undocumented Latinos hurt the economy, lower wages, compete for jobs with native Americans, and disproportionately increase crime. But UC Davis Economics Professor Giovanni Peri (in a 2007 study by the Public Policy Institute, based on U.S. census data) found that undocumented Latinos aid the economy, boost wages of American citizens, and do not take their jobs.** Another study (by the Immigration Policy Center, also based on U.S. Census data) found that incarceration rates of undocumented Latinos were five times less than native born Latinos.

They claim that undocumented border crossers disproportionately use hospital emergency facilities. This is not the case. These undocumented are 50% less likely to use emergency rooms (study by the *Archives of Internal Medicine*).

State and local government, particularly in the border states, do disproportionately bear a financial burden by the presence of undocumented Latinos in their midst. Why is this true? These undocumented pay sales and property taxes (as renters) to state and local governments, add to the economy, aid the profits of employers by offering cheap labor, and keep prices lower for consumers.

Also the federal government collects income and Social Security taxes from undocumented Latinos. But they do not share in such a way that would compensate states and localities for their costs.

---

* U.S Immigration and Customs Enforcement does not seek the deportation of very many undocumented. They seldom seek the deportion of any over-stayers (the majority of undocumented). Overstayers are from all continents. Besides, deporting them would be too expensive.

U.S. Immigration and Customs Enforcement also seldom seeks the deportation of agricultural employees. What are the reasons? Agricultural employers make large contributions to election campaigns of politicians. Also Enforcement does not want to be responsible for crops rotting in the fields. Furthermore, they would have great difficulty replacing them with the unemployed. American unemployed would rather collect unemployment compensation (if eligible). In any event, very few, if any, would like to move to Arizona or the Central Valley of California for part-time poorly paid jobs, working in the hot sun. Not enough other people would be interested in the jobs.

Immigration and Customs Enforcement very seldom raids sweatshops. Americans do not want to work in sweatshops. They very rarely cite the great numbers of potential voters who hire undocumented Latinos as maids, nannies, gardeners, and etc. (not good politics and too expensive). Enforcement mostly raids construction sites, factories, and slaughterhouses because Americans can be found to take these much more highly paid jobs.

**They do sometimes compete for jobs with undocumented Latinos who entered the U.S. earlier, and with blacks.

TENENTS OF NATIVISTS

Nativists do not oppose undocumented Latino border crossers because of all the burdens they supposedly place on American society. Their purpose in making these assertions is to seek popular support for their white supremacy stance. *

What drives Nativists in California currently is their goal of halting and reversing the browning of California (and the U.S.). In California, they particularly dread what they see as the Mexicanization of the state.

Nativists' long-term plan has always been to oppose any immigration which threatens the American nation as they see it, a singular predominantly Euro-American English speaking culture. They appeal to tribalism.

But Americans are not a tribe. America is a nation of immigrants..

What Nativists really fear is a path to citizenship for undocumented, or for federal labor importation *braceros.* They also dread large scale legal Latino immigration, and citizenship for undocumented offspring who are born in the U.S. These latter are clearly guaranteed citizenship by the Constitution and practice. Offspring of undocumented will not have to wait Nativists feel compelled to block as many Latinos as possible from U.S. citizen-

They feel compelled to block as many Latinos as possible from U.S. citizenship** They do not want them voting in American elections.

It is understandable that Nativists are desperate not to be an electoral minority. They have been in the forefront of efforts to impose cultural uniformity on minorities, and frequently in the past 200 or so years Nativists were leading participants in the maltreatment of American Indians, blacks, Asians, Irish, Germans, Italians, Mexicans, Jews and Catholics, etc.

Of course racism is a part of the opposition to undocumented Latinos. But most Californians (and Americans) are not racists, and those who hold the tenents of white supremacists would not win their favor. Being not correctly informed, they fear for their jobs (understandably). They favor border security.***

---

* There is also xenophobia. It means fear and hatred of strangers or foreigners, or anything that is strange or foreign. Webster's Collegiate Dictionary.

**The U.S. Bureau of Citizenship and Immigration Services has also been blocking legal Latino immigrants from citizenship. Citizenship fees which were $95 in 1998, and $400 in 2006 were $675 in 2008. These high fees effectively block poor Latino immigrants (and other immigrants) from citizenship and thus from voting.

***A tactic now used by many proponents of a stricter border enforcement on the U.S.-Mexican border is to insist that after 9/11, they fear that terrorists could enter over the heavily guarded U.S-Mexican border. (In the more than five years since 9/11 none have been apprehended.). On the other hand, some of the 9/11 terrorists were overstayers. Furthermore, they do not object to the practically unguarded U.S.-Canada border (a much more likely entry point for terrorists).

A FENCE ON THE U.S. BORDER A SOLUTION?

Obviously, securing the border and deporting 12 million undocumented Latinos would not solve our current labor deficit and the much greater shortage to come. Also, securing the border would mean more overstayers. And it would keep illegal entrants from going to their homes across the border. Actually, the number of undocumented entering the U.S. is generally dependent on the number of jobs available here.

But securing the border could greatly help with the thousands of American licensed gun shops close to the U.S.-Mexico border who sell guns (including automatic weapons) which Mexican drug cartels use against the Mexican army and police.

USC International Relations Professor Pamela Starr found that about 4,000 Mexicans were killed in the drug wars in 2008. The drug wars have been going on for about seven years.

More Mexicans have been killed in the drug wars than Americans killed in Iraq and Afghanistan combined. Meanwhile, the illegal drug traffic to the U.S. flourishes.

Illegal drugs are illegal entrants to the U.S. Illegal guns are illegal entrants to Mexico.

A MASSIVE LABOR IMPORTION PROGRAM A SOLUTION?

If the goal is to stop undocumented Latino entry humanely and effectively, the U.S. and Mexican governments could bring into being an inviting option (a form of guest worker program). Fifty years ago we had such a massive program, the Labor Importation Program.

In 1956, there were 445,000 labor importation *braceros* working in the U.S., and the border was secured (See Figure 1). And while in California in 1954, over 540,000 undocumented were apprehended, in 1956, only slightly over 23,000 were (See Figure 2).

With the Labor Importation Program at its peak in 1956, our 1,200 member Border Patrol sealed the border. Today, with 18,000 personnel, some fences, thousands of Reservists, and with much better surveillance equipment, it can not.

Figure 1

APPREHENSIONS OF UNDOCUMENTED
MEXICAN ENTRANTS: 1954-1956

14

FISCAL YEAR

FIGURE 2

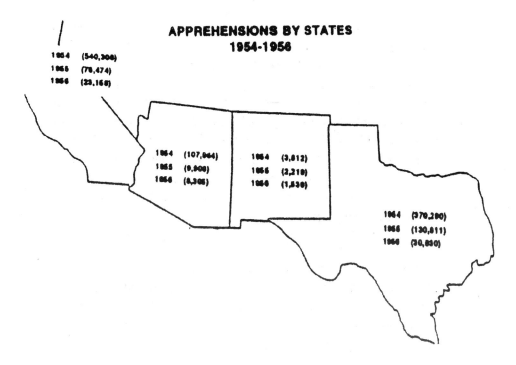

APPREHENSIONS BY STATES
1954-1956

1954   (540,306)
1955   (78,474)
1956   (23,155)

1954   (107,864)
1955   (9,900)
1956   (8,305)

1954   (3,812)
1955   (2,219)
1956   (1,539)

1954   (370,290)
1955   (130,811)
1956   (30,830)

SOURCE: STATISTICS BRANCH, IMMIGRATION
AND NATURALIZATION SERVICE

A MUCH LARGER LEGAL ADMISSION A SOLUTION?

President George W. Bush said in 2006, that"...there is an easy way to lessen illegal immigration. It is to alter the laws so more people can enter legally."

Legal immigration has advantages. Legal immigration could mean admitting workers as needed. Criminals could be rejected, people with communicable diseases could be kept out (until cured).

But undocumented Latino border crossers might be better than legal immigrants. They would probably be younger, stronger, and more venturesome (willing to risk their lives in a difficult crossing).

NEEDED: A COMPREHENSIVE IMMIGRATION LAW*

We need a comprehensive immigration reform which not only deals with the undocumented question, but also with legal immigration, and the immigration of HI-Bs, very talented foreign workers (i.e., engineers and computer scientists) who would be added to the U.S. workforce. We are not competing effectively with the European Union and Canada for H1-Bs, maintaining low quotas and high fees, $5,000 for H1-Bs.

CALIFORNIA'S EXAMPLE

In 1994, older white voters struck out at undocumented Latinos by passing Proposition 187 (an attempt to limit public services to undocumented Latinos). Undocumented overstayers were not targeted. But today, Californians are much more accepting of undocumented Latinos.

Because of the high cost of living in California, "illegal" entrants have been in great numbers migrating across the Mexican border to many other states. This has caused voters in other states to react as California voters did in 1994, tending to look upon the undocumented as a burden, rather than future caretakers. These attitudes should change when voters in these states become more aware of the current and coming labor shortages and the greying of their populations.

---

* Passage of a comprehensive immigration law for undocumented Latino border crossers with a path to legal residence and citizenship will probably not come soon. President Obama's priorities are the economy, tax cuts for the "middle class," health care, energy, and education. It seems he will not want to promote soon an immigration law which would mean contesting with Nativists and organized labor.

He is probably going to reward Latinos who voted for him (67% nationwide) by appointing Latinos to high profile positions (perhaps even to the Supreme Court) and by stopping workplace raids to catch undocumented Latinos. But with the eventual passage of a comprehensive law (perhaps early in his second term) .

THE SQUANDERING OF AMERICA, AND DEALING WITH THE CLEAR AND PRESENT ECONOMIC DANGER—THE RECESSION OF 2008

CALIFORNIA'S INFLUENCE ON FEDERAL DECISIONS

The Governor of California is probably second only to the president of the U.S. in political weight. His influence can be epic. He can animate the people of California to a compelling idea, cause, or plan which gets not only local, but national and even international attention — and frequent emulation. For instance, Governor Edmond G. (Pat) Brown pushed through a mammoth state water project, an extensive highway system, and a scheme of higher education — all parts of an infrastructure which laid the base for years of economic prosperity in California.

But the influence of the California Governor (and the state's legislature) on many matters Californians are very concerned about is generally marginal. The economy of California, for instance, depends largely on the health of the U.S. economy, federal spending, the value of the dollar, federal taxation, federal borrowing, immigration, wars, the regulation of banks and Wall Street, the interest rate established by the Federal Reserve Board, the solvency of national banks, military build-ups, imperialist ventures, foreign affairs, fuel supply, inflation and deflation, outsourcing, and global trends, etc.

But California's congressional delegation (55 in number), bigger than any other state's, does influence federal decisions. It largely joined with other congresspersons and presidents in squandering America with debts and deficits.

CALIFORNIA'S SHARE OF THE FEDERAL DEBT AND DEFICITS

A study by Godhale and Smetters about seven years ago (commissioned by U.S. Secretary of the Treasury Paul O'Neal) revealed that the debt and federal deficits of the U.S. amounted to $45 trillion. In 2007, Goldman Sachs reported that debt and unfunded deficits were up to $59 trillion. *USA Today* found (2009), that the debt and deficits are about $69 trillion and rapidly growing. You might ask how much is California's share of the federal debt and deficits. It is about $10 trillion, and growing.

Could we Americans easily pay off the federal debt and deficits ? USA TODAY calculated (2007) that to pay off the federal debt and deficits every U.S. household (including, of course, Californians) would have to pay $31,000 per year for the next 75 years.* This quotation is taken directly from USA TODAY, June 29, 2007.

WHY DO WE HAVE MORE THAN A $10.5 TRILLION FEDERAL DEBT?

Military build-ups and the Iraq War are chiefly responsible for the current national debt. Military build-ups and wars also mean that money is not available for Social Security, Medicare, and other social programs. The largest

---

*In 2009, it would take about 80 years.

peacetime build-up came during the Ronald Reagan presidency, a build-up costing $1.2. trillion and financed by borrowing. President Reagan sought a military that could further American imperialism.*

Reagan also sought what Charles Mair called an "Empire of Consumption." Reagan thought enlarged popular consumption in America was a key to a stronger American economy and the securing of a greater American empire by making foreign nations more dependent on sales to the U.S. During his administration, both the American people and nation took to borrowing. Thus, America became a debtor nation with a negative trade balance.

Reagan was also a big spender. He rang up huge budget deficits. His predecessor, President Jimmy Carter, had average deficits of $59 billion a year, Reagan had average deficits of $210.6 billion a year. He separated military spending from the budget. President George W. Bush followed his example.** He also shared Reagan's belief that business is best when not strictly regulated by government. Reagan, like Bush, wanted an American imperium in the Persian Gulf. As Andrew Bacevich said "...History will hold George W. Bush primarily responsible for the disastrous Iraq War of 2003. But if that war had a godfather, it was Ronald Reagan."***

When the Iraq War commenced in 2003, and because of costly military build-ups, the U.S. had 9,000 M1 Abrams tanks. The world had no equivalents. The U.S. had 11 "super carrier" battle groups and three types of stealth bombers. The world had none. The U.S. had more than 700 military bases in more than 130 countries (an empire of bases). All of this made the U.S. the strongest empire in the history of the world, weapons wise.

But the empire was built on credit. Today, it has far fewer troops. It has a citizenry made up of ardent shoppers, not militarists. It does not want a draft, has little staying power in an elective war, likes its wars to be "free wars" (no taxes), does not like American casualties, and increasingly sees that recent expansions of the empire weakens the U.S.

The U.S. sees advantages in never calling itself an empire. The media are complicit. Thus, it is not surprising that, against all evidence, very few Americans believe that the U.S. is an empire. The whole world knows that it is. Why is it that the American people are so myopic? Is it as Francis Bacon said in 1620, "People believe what they prefer." ?

But remember, the American people are not anti-war, they are anti-defeat. George McGovern learned this the hard way. As the Democratic Party candidate for president in 1972, he called for Americans to come home from the Vietnam War. He won in one state. Incumbent President Richard Nixon won in 49. All politicians took notice. They still do.

---

*His confrontation with the U.S.S.R. was a clash of empires, as was World War I, World War II, the Korean War, and the Vietnam War.

**President George W. Bush's debacle in Iraq caused thousands of deaths. It also cost trillions of dollars. In 2008, President Bush spent $600 billions on the war. Nobel Prize winner, Joseph Stiglitz, found the cost of the Iraq War to be $3 trillion (See Joseph Stiglitz and Linda J. Bilmes, *The Three Trillion Dollar War: The True Cost of the Iraq Conflict.)* W. W. Norton, March 3, 2008.). This figure of Stiglitz's will increase.

***Andrew J. Bacevich, *The Limits of Power.* (New York:Henry Holt and Company, p. 49.) .

WHY DO WE HAVE A $59 TRILLION FEDERAL DEFICIT?

In 1935, when the Social Security system was enacted, there were 42 workers to support each Social Security retiree. Now there are about three workers to support Social Security and Medicare retirees.

In the first place, most workers did not live to be 65 in 1935. Today, Americans are living longer. According to the U.S. Census Bureau, the number of persons over 65 today are expected to double between now and 2030. Eighty-five year olds are expected to number 21 million by 2050. Almost 30% of the costs of Medicare is during the last year of life.

Also important is the low birth rates of white non-Latino women in the U.S. since 1964. Currently, their birth rate is only 1.6. The replacement rate is 2.1.* Conversely, the high birth rates after World War II (1946-1964) produced the so-called "Baby Boomer" generation of 78 million. This was the greatest generational imbalance in U.S. history.

WHAT ARE SOME THINGS THAT COULD BE DONE ABOUT THE DEFICITS AND DEBT?

We need young immigrants to return some measure of balance to the U.S. population. The Census Bureau said 10 million by 2010. It seems that this will have to wait for the end of the recession of 2008.

We have a more immediate need for certain H1-Bs (i.e., very highly skilled engineers and computer scientists) added to the workforce.** We are not competing effectively with the European Union and Canada for H1-Bs. This is one of the reasons companies are moving out of the U.S.

Also, we could raise the age of retirement for Social Security (and Medicare) to 67 or even 70. Also, due to the recession, many workers will choose later retirements.

We could also raise much money for Social Security coffers if we taxed persons earning over $102,000 (the current limit). The Economic Policy Institute estimated that taxing the incomes of the top six percent of wage earners by 6.2 percent (same as lower wage earners pay) would eliminate 75 percent of the shortfall predicted for Social Security funds. Please note that Social Security provides for a number of social programs. Thus, it is a social system, in addition to being a retirement system for contributors.

As for Medicare, we could cut payments to doctors and hospitals. Not too wise, there will be a shortage of doctors, and many hospitals are already going bankrupt. Also, we could increase costs of supplementary insurance to recipients. But attempted substantial increase in costs or making cuts to recipients would meet with strong opposition from older voters, making the chances of higher costs or cuts to recipients remote. Another problem, George Will wrote in December, 2008, that Medicaid (medical care for indigents) may cost more than Medicare. Medicare's deficits are about $35 trillion. If Medicaid will cost more than Medicare, we are then looking at deficits and debts of about $90 trillion.

---

*This is not just an American problem. Western Europe has low birth rates. Spain's is the lowest, less than 1.0.

**Almost 2/3 of the P.h.Ds in engineering graduates in the U.S. are foreign students.

THE ROLE OF CONGRESS

Congress should have been setting aside funds for the past 30 to 40 years for Social Security and Medicare, which Californians (and all Americans), depend upon. Congress persons did not talk about the $59 trillion unfunded deficits. They caused it, and do not want to admit it. To pay for it by enormous taxes, very deeply cutting services, refusing to fund elective wars, or opposing the military-industrial complex's budget requests — all of these actions would very likely end their political careers.* So they borrow or otherwise delay payments.**

CONGRESS AND SPECIAL INTERESTS

Congresspersons regularly cast their votes for special interests who contribute heavily to their election campaigns. If you read President Lincoln's call for government "of the people, by the people, and for the people" you might get legislation passed to strictly limit special interest contributions. You would likely find that the U.S. Supreme Court, which did nothing when George W. Bush shredded the constitution, would likely give you a large dose of judicial hegemony and rule the reform unconstitutional. If you then got a similar constitutional amendment enacted in California, you would probably get another large dose of judicial hegemony when the courts rule the constitutional amendment unconstitutional.

THIS IS HOW THE CALIFORNIA CONSTITUTION IS AMENDED BY POPULAR VOTE

PROPOSAL

Amendment Proposed Through Initiative Petition Containing Signatures of Registered Voters Equal in Number to 8 Percent of All Votes Cast for All Candidates for Governor at the Preceding Gubernatorial Election

APPROVAL

By a Majority of Voters Voting

AN AGED UNCLE SAM
ALTHOUGH NOT PERFECT, HE DID NOT DESERVE TO HAVE HIS NATION SQUANDERED

*President Eisenhower warned us of the military industrial complex.

** There is a limit to our borrowing power. The time will come, but we do not know when, that we can not borrow sufficient money. Perhaps it will result from a U.S. default on domestic or international debt, or concern of nations about the value of the falling dollar, or a falling out with major bond holders, who now hold some considerable sway over us.

THE RECESSION OF 2008

WHO CAUSED THE RECESSION?

Paul Krugman, our newest Nobel Prize-winner, in his last sentence of his 2009 book on the 2008 Recession, stated that "... the only structural obstacles to the world's prosperity are the absolute doctrines that clutter the minds of men." He dismissed claims that the American peoples' proclivity to spend beyond their means caused the recession.* "... The American public (he said) had no idea what was going on..." The American people were urged to borrow, to build an apparently stronger economy, to borrow and spend so the government could build a greater empire.

He asserted that "...the people who did know what was going on thought that deregulation of the economy was a great idea." You do not need to be a Nobel Prize-winner to see that when only about two percent of average Californians could buy an average priced house, that the bubble was going to burst.**

Who then caused the Recession? At fault were Republican presidents, Republican congress persons, Democratic congress persons who were complicit and exercised no real oversight, federal "regulators" who did not regulate, Alan Greenspan, Chairman of the Federal Reserve, who opposed all proposals for a prudent regulation of the financial system, greedy shadow banks, greedy Wall Streeters, Fannie Mae and Freddie Mac, and loan originators.

WHY DID THE RECESSION OCCUR?

The primary reason is that home buyers and creditors all believed or acted on the assumption that house prices would continue to increase, that houses could be sold at any time with a sizeable profit. (How wrong they were.) The Republican administration pushed this idea, believing that homeowners would more likely vote Republican.

Most destructive were sub prime loans, so called liar loans, many of which involved criminal fraud, or were unwise in the extreme. Mostly the sub prime loans were made to minorities. (They did not need sub prime loans. They needed good jobs with good pay).

Sub prime loans were made to buyers often with nothing down, without proper credit, and without evidence of ability to pay the loan. It was assumed that these houses would increase in value and the buyer could then refinance the loan, or sell the house, pay off the mortgage, and make a profit.

Loan originators got paid their commissions for the original sale and were home free because they typically sold the mortgage to a financial institution (called a shadow bank). Shadow banks used them to falsify their bottom lines so that their stocks would rise and they would greatly profit. At peak, the financial services dominated the S&P index. It was a giant Ponzi scheme.

---

* The American people, living as they do in the present, had $2 trillion in credit card debt and a savings rate that was about the same as during the Great Depression. Americans always spent too much during times of apparent prosperity and save money during downturns. This is just the opposite of what they should do.

** Now about 20% can.

Many homeowners regularly borrowed parts of their home equities. When the housing bubble burst, the value of homes dropped "nearly 50%" in California. They saw that the mortgage on their home was more than their houses were worth on the market (even if they paid 20% down and did not draw on their equity). Many homeowners walked away from their homes or had them foreclosed. Some workers lost as much as 50% of the value of their 401(ks). Many others lost their jobs as well.

The loss of their homes was a personal tragedy for them, but also a very big loss for their mortgage holders. Creditors sometimes got back only about half of the original value of the loans. The shadow banks lost over $1 trillion. This caused a great liquidity problem. Also, even after banks were rescued from bankruptcy by the federal government, they would not (or could not) make loans needed to drive the economy. People without loans could not buy automobiles and other costly items.

Republican attempts to refinance some banks and rescue others did not work because the money given had no regulation. Also, when the Republican administration lowered taxes, it did no good, nor did their first grant to General Motors — no restrictions.

WHAT TO DO ABOUT THE RECESSION OF 2008

Using a pragmatic approach, we will examine what worked or did not work in various recessions, with particular reference to the Great American Depression of the 1930s

FIRST, WHAT NOT TO DO

Do not raise taxes. Do not try to balance the budget. Do not try solving the problem with too little government investment. Do not inaugurate a tariff or a buy American plan. These would boomerang. Republicans passed a tariff early in the depression. It did not work. (But during the Great Depression, Republicans helped President Roosevelt. Very few Republicans are currently helping President Obama.). Do not delay government intervention, the recession will worsen with any delay. Do not cut taxes for small businesses. They will not expand because of the tax cuts, but will wait until large numbers of customers arrive in their stores with large amounts of money to spend. Do not reduce taxes for middle wage earners. They will simply save the money or payoff debts. They do this in hard times. China was aware of this when they embarked on a program to get people spending. They gave them substantial dated coupons so they could buy any items of their choice — a far better idea.*

Do not reduce job creating programs during the recession. President Roosevelt tried this in 1937. The Depression returned. Do not rescue banks with billions of dollars without exacting strict regulations. Do not be afraid of the N-word, nationalization of banking (temporarily). When the banking system is rescued, it can be reformed and strictly supervised.**

---

* Dang Xiaoping launched China on the road to capitalism in 1978, two years after the radical Maoists' defeat. China is now a very successful capitalist state. So there is no problem copying Chinese solutions. China is building a bullet train (350 miles an hour) to its eastern provinces.

** President Obama says he will raise taxes on people making over $250,000. Then he also wants to reduce the costs of the Iraq War, avoid perennial federal deficits, establish a health plan, and heavily finance the development of alternative energy sources.

SECOND, WHAT TO DO

Government spending to create jobs should be large enough. (It is far better to spend too much than too little.). As soon as possible, reduce war costs. Spend on renewable energies. Reduce drastically the miles per gallon of gas driven vehicles. Vastly increase mass transit in cities. (Expect oil companies and auto makers to oppose this, as they successfully lobbied against mass transit in large cities when freeways were built.).

If we really want to get out of the Recession of 2008, we should do what got us out of the Great Depression of the 1930s. It was World War II government spending. Instead of five % of the Gross National Product given to President Obama to do the job, the government spent up to 70% of GNP for 1944. (By 1942, 52% of GNP was spent.).

The government built a tremendous infrastructure which provided the nation's enormous prosperity, achieving an unemployment rate of only one % by 1944. Could we do this again? Could we repair today's rotting infrastructure? Of course we could. It would completely solve the unemployment problem.

The American Society of Civil Engineers described out current American infrastructure as dreadful, and said it would require a $2.2 trillion investment over 5 years to put it back in shape. Bob Herbert, of the *New York Times* said that if this is not done, "The U.S. will still be a nation with a pathetic mid-twentieth century infrastructure struggling to make it in a dynamic 21st century world. It is a blueprint for sustained national decline." On the other hand, with a new and aggressive policy we could greatly reduce unemployment and usher in a robust America. We could pay down the deficit. We could, with a large import of younger workers, greatly correct our generational imbalance. We could then help reverse the years of squandering of our great nation.

2 CHAPTER

CALIFORNIA'S CONSTITUTIONAL SCHEME

LEGACIES OF THE CALIFORNIA INDIANS

Though these native Californians placed little emphasis on government, they conveyed a significant legacy. Engaging in hunting, fishing and gathering to sustain themselves, they became skilled naturalists and behaved exemplarily towards their environment. They also lived peacefully--without destroying each other. Totally submerged, the California Indians did not influence the development of California's early constitutional schemes.

Spanish exploration of the coastal area above Mexico began in 1542, when an expedition led by Juan Cabrillo "discovered" San Diego Bay. Myriad expeditions followed, but not until 1769, when Gaspar de Portolá and Fray Junípero Serra established a mission and a fort at the current *situs* of San Diego, did Spanish occupation become actuality. Spain was trying to block Russian and British expansion.

The Spanish Franciscan Fathers eventually constructed 21 *missions*, the northernmost at Sonoma, to train and preserve the Indians, who were to be a basic element of the society. *Presidios* (forts) were built to secure the missions (which were agricultural *pueblos* [towns] as well as churches), and separate pueblos sprang up along the mission trails. These institutions were the beginnings of many California cities.

The Spanish era ended in 1822, when Mexico (after winning independence from Spain in 1821) began to rule California. Between 1834 and 1846, it secularized the missions, thus essentially ending the Franciscan design, and in the so-called Laws of 1837, provided a government for California, with a governor appointed by the central government in Mexico City, a popularly elected seven member legislature, and a judicial structure similar to our present one, but with the *alcalde* — a composite of local judge, mayor, and chief of police — the dominant figure.

Though Mexican rule brought to California concepts of *republicanism*, *representation*, and *constitutionalism*, both our Mexican and Spanish heritages are (like our Indian), principally in areas other than government. For instance, Spanish language place names survive, the local vocabulary has been influenced, and certain trends in the architecture and furniture of the Mexican era persist, as does the cuisine. Also, land titles rest on Spanish and Mexican bases, and California community property laws are founded on Spanish law.

LEGACY OF THE AMERICAN PERIOD (1846-1849)

The so-called American period, inaugurated early in the general war with Mexico (1846-1848), when the annexation of California was declared by President James Polk, conveyed a meaningful legacy: resentment by Americans arriving during American military rule, of the incongruent *alcalde* governance. Carried over from the Mexican period, it violated the principle of separation of powers, a custom these Americans already cherished, and increasingly enshrined. Not surprisingly, the California Constitution (unlike the U.S. Constitution) includes a specific statement of separation of governmental powers.

Inexperienced in lawmaking the framers relied chiefly on the constitution of Iowa—most modern in the West—and to a lesser extent on New York's recently revised constitution. Also, the weight of other state constitutions, as well as of the U.S. Constitution, may be seen. It incorporated the entire federal Bill of Rights.

CALIFORNIA'S FIRST CONSTITUTION (1849)

Certain good may be said of the first Constitution. It was a simple and clear statement of basic principles and procedures, and popular approval was overwhelming — 12,872 for, 811 against. Even Congress did not derogate it, though complaining about methods followed — particularly the call to the convention, and the fashioning of a state instead of a territorial government (which went into effect immediately, before admission to statehood — mostly to check lawlessness). But eventually it was criticized for not limiting the Legislature's power to tax and spend, and because under it taxes had become "unduly high" and corporations exercised "too much control" over California's government, particularly the Legislature.

The 1849 Constitution was replaced not so much because it was a flawed document, but owing to severe economic and social troubles of the 1870's. Long past were the lush days of the gold rush; the Comstock Lode (mostly silver) had begun its final decline. Unemployment climbed as thousands of Chinese railroad workers entered (upon completion of the transcontinental railroad in 1869). In one year, a record 22,000 arrived in San Francisco alone.

DENIS KEARNEY AND CALIFORNIA'S PRESENT CONSTITUTION (1879)

In the late 1870's, workers flocked to the newly organized Kearneyite (Workingmen's) Party. Headed by Denis Kearney, a County Cork, Ireland immigrant, it opposed private importation of cheap alien labor, corruption in government, dishonest banking, plutocratic control of California by corporations, and land monopoly.* It demanded constitutional change. As the depression of the 1870's worsened, farmers (suffering particularly from the monopolistic methods of banks, big landowners, and railroads) joined the Kearneyites' clamor for reform. In 1877, a call for a constitutional convention was approved by the voters.

Kearney's specific program was hardly radical by today's standards. But Kearney's fiery rhetoric, and his recommendation that "Every workingman should get a musket," frightened conservatives, much as Shays's Rebellion had alarmed the Founding Fathers of the U.S. Constitution.

---

*Earlier, as King of the San Francisco Hoodlums, Kearney powerfully opposed Oriental immigration and Oriental contract labor. But he said many times that California workers should work as hard as the Chinese.

Denis Kearney. All his speeches conveyed this message:
The capitalists must create jobs for the workers.

Fearing the Kearneyites might control the convention, Democrats and Republicans dropped their labels and became "Nonpartisans." In a further design, conservatives got an additional 32 delegates-at-large seats added to the convention. All were won by Nonpartisans. By then, every newspaper in the state was opposing Kearney.

Of the 152 convention delegates, 51 were Workingmen. Eleven were Republicans, ten Democrats, two Independents, and 78 Nonpartisan. Most (57) were lawyers or farmers (39).

The draft constitution restricted the Legislature, particularly in finance; exposed corporations to much more severe regulation; and directed the Legislature to deter Chinese immigration.

Clearly, the Constitution of 1879 (our present Constitution) did not inaugurate wholesale reform. It incorporated just enough of Kearney's agenda to smother his movement, and otherwise mostly embellished the Constitution of 1849, making it more specific and detailed — actually tripling its length. Major reform was not to be achieved until decades later — with Hiram Johnson and the Progressives.

Few were completely satisfied with the draft constitution. Conservatives condemned it as communistic, and workingmen were incensed by its scanty fare for labor. Strongest support was from the Grangers, who felt (mistakenly) it would mean lower freight rates and taxes. Approval was by a margin of only 11,000 of a total popular vote of 145,000.

Demand for political change diminished greatly with the return of prosperity to California in 1880. By the end of that year the Workingmen's Party had nearly disappeared.

Hiram Johnson. His objectivity, however fractional, was remarkable, and he seemed to have a vision of a greater democracy.

Photograph courtesy of the California State Library

CONSTITUTIONAL AND POLITICAL LEGACY OF HIRAM JOHNSON AND THE PROGRESSIVES

From the decline of Kearneyism until the rise in the early years of the twentieth century of the California Progressive Movement, California politics was dominated by the Southern Pacific Railroad (SP). It used its political power to control the Railroad Commission, maintain its exorbitant rate structure and its transportation monopoly, and amass for itself much of the state's resources. But following particularly abusive tactics of its political machine in the 1906 gubernatorial election, sentiment against SP quickened.

Voters struck hard at entrenched political leadership, approving overwhelmingly (in 1908) a constitutional amendment permitting the direct primary system, thus ending the convention system of nomination which had been used so successfully by SP. In 1910, they elected as Governor, Progressive Republican Hiram Johnson, who had promised to throw SP out of the Republican Party and out of California politics.

Aided by large majorities in both houses of the legislature, the Progressives set out not to institute a particular version of social and economic justice, but to make California government more democratic and efficient, itself a worthy enterprise. The fundamental framework of government in California is today the result of Progressive efforts.

Among their more consequential reforms were these: reanimating the Railroad Commission and placing every privately owned utility under its jurisdiction; writing woman suffrage into the Constitution; promoting worker's compensation; further weakening political party organizations by making local government, judicial, and school elections nonpartisan, and requiring that names of candidates for partisan offices appear on the ballot by office rather than by party blocs; extending the civil service; instituting procedures enabling voters to *recall* any elected official from office, and through *referendum* to block statutes from taking effect; and enacting conservation programs to protect the state's natural resources. Ostensibly the Progressives' most momentous reform was the institution in 1911 of direct legislation — *the initiative* — enabling the voters to initiate and enact laws or constitutional amendments, a still powerful popular tool.

But one of the principal reforms of the Progressives is hotly debated currently, a constitutionally required 2/3 vote of both houses of the Legislature to enact a state budget. Progressives required the 2/3 majority (still a constitutional requirement) because they wanted to make the budget bipartisan. But in practice this has meant perennial gridlock and, perhaps more importantly nearly always neither the Democrats nor the Republicans are responsible for what will be done, and for the funds that are spent to do it.

Unlike the working class Kearneyites, California Progressives were individualists and were mostly middle or upper economic class. While criticizing both politically organized capital and labor, they had much greater bias against organized labor. Today, Progressivism provides a base for liberalism in California.

Although the decision-making processes of the federal and California governments are mostly separate and distinct, there are significant affinities. For instance, both follow a pattern of limited representative government, a written constitution, amendment clauses, civilian supremacy, separated powers, checks and balances, a bicameral legislature, a popularly elected executive, and a bill of rights.

HOW CALIFORNIA'S CONSTITUTION AND THE U.S. CONSTITUTION DIFFER

CALIFORNIA'S CONSTITUTION

1. Unitary Form
2. Residual Powers
3. Plural Executive
4. Legislature Shares Power With Voters (Initiative and Referendum)
5. A Combination of Appointment and Election of Judges
6. Relatively Rigid and Detailed Constitution
7. Amendment Easy. Voters May Participate Directly

U.S. CONSTITUTION

1. Federal Form
2. Delegated Powers
3. Single Chief Executive
4. Congress Granted All Legislative Power
5. Judges Appointed by the President
6. Flexible Constitution Limited to Fundamentals
7. Amendment Difficult. No Direct Popular Input

HOW CALIFORNIA'S CONSTITUTION CHANGES
INFORMAL MODIFICATIONS

Like its federal counterpart, California's Constitution is modified *informally* by custom and by interpretations of the executive, legislative, and judicial branches.

FOUR METHODS OF FORMALLY AMENDING THE CALIFORNIA CONSTITUTION

PROPOSAL	APPROVAL
Amendment Proposed by 2/3 Vote of the Members of the Assembly and the Senate OR Amendment Proposed Through Initiative Petition Containing Signatures of Registered Voters Equal in Number to 8 Percent of All Votes Cast for All Candidates for Governor at the Preceding Gubernatorial Election OR Amendments Based on Recommendations of a Revisory Commission and Approved by 2/3 Vote of the Members of the Assembly and the Senate ~~OR Constitutional Convention, Proposed By 2/3 Vote of Members of the Assembly and the Senate~~	By a Majority of Voters Voting

Among the more significant *formal amendments* was the legislatively proposed amendment which in 1911, incorporated the initiative process into the California Constitution giving legislative power to the voters (previously an exclusive prerogative of the Legislature); a 1922 initiative amendment vested in the Governor power to construct and submit to the Legislature a budget for the entire state government and to reduce or eliminate items of appropriation (thus affecting substantially the relative potency of the Governor); a 1962 constitutional amendment specifically empowered the Legislature to propose revisions of the Constitution (previously accomplished only by constitutional convention); and Proposition 140, in 1990, limiting legislative terms may have further

CONSTITUTION REVISION COMMISSION'S PRINCIPAL PROPOSALS*

- Candidates for Governor and Lieutenant Governor to run as a ticket (as do candidates for President and Vice President of the U.S.), thus eliminating the counterproductive political rivalry when the Governor and Lieutenant Governor belong to different parties.
- The now elective State Treasurer, State Superintendent of Public Instruction, and State Insurance Commissioner to be gubernatorial appointees (subject to legislative confirmation).
- The Governor and legislators to be subjected to monetary penalties should they not enact a state budget on time.
- A truly balanced state budget (instead of the current constitutional mandate that the Governor *submit* a balanced budget, but *not* requiring the Legislature to *enact* one).
- A *two-year* balanced state budget (instead of the current one-year budget), periodic revisions to insure balance throughout the fiscal period, and no rollovers of deficits from one year to another.
- A simple majority vote in each house to pass a state budget (instead of the current two-thirds of each house requirement — which results in perennial gridlock).
- Members of *both houses* be permitted to serve *three four year terms* (thus relaxing Prop. 140 term limits).
- Allow property tax increases (now prohibited by Prop. 13) to support local public schools, by a two-thirds vote of the local electorate, and permit a countywide sales tax increase of one half percent for public schools on endorsement by a *majority* of county voters (instead of the two-thirds vote required by Prop. 13).
- Provide for citizens charter commissions in each county to examine and amend overlapping and conflicting jurisdiction of counties, cities, and special districts.
- Give local governments strong new home rule powers, and new taxing powers to pay for local services.

    * The Constitution Revision Commission was composed of 23 members appointed by the Governor and the leaders of the Legislature.

weakened the Legislature relative to the Governor and thus (some feel) worked a constitutional revision. However, in October of 1991, the California Supreme Court, ruling on Proposition 140, rejected the claim of a constitutional revision, holding that the essential powers of the Legislature were unaffected.

CONSTITUTIONAL REVISION IN PRACTICE

The 1966 *constitutional revision* removed about 16,000 words from the Constitution (which had ballooned to more than ten times the size of the national document), provided annual general sessions of the Legislature, required the Legislature to pass conflict of interest legislation, and empowered the Governor to reorganize the executive branch. The voters rejected a yet more sweeping constitutional revision in 1968, but revisions in 1972, 1974 and 1978, though less ambitious, removed needless and obsolete language, reducing the size of the document by about one-third.

WHY NOT TODAY AN ENTIRELY NEW CALIFORNIA CONSTITUTION?

We might ask why in this age of change we do not change constitutions — write a new California constitution to replace our about 125 year-old document. In 1934, the legislature did ask the voters if they wanted to have a constitutional convention called. The majority voted "Yes." However, no convention has been called. Why? The same basic reason applies now as in the 1930's. Many features in our Constitution favor powerful groups in the state. These groups are content to see parts of the Constitution that do not interest them revised, but oppose altering or eliminating those parts they succeeded in having inserted.

Furthermore, *a convention* having, of course, full powers to draft an entirely *new constitution* could, for instance, mandate a unicameral state legislature, or abolish the 2/3 rule for the approval of the budget or the raising of taxes. But Governor Schwarzenegger and many citizens groups want a constitutional convention. This could be done by popular intiative. It could also be done by a 2/3 vote by the California Senate and Assembly, but this is very unlikely. Its work could be approved by a *majority of the voters voting*, the California Legislature having no role in the ratification process. Little wonder the Legislature has not again asked the voters if they want a new constitution.

3 CHAPTER

LIBERTIES AND RIGHTS (DENIALS AND EXTENSIONS)

The major sources of liberties and rights of Californians are the California and the U.S. constitutions, and California and federal laws (and treaties). Enforcement is by California courts and by federal courts, both of which honor U.S. Supreme Court precedents.

California courts also commonly cite in their decisions comparable clauses contained in *both* the constitutions of California and of the U.S. (e.g., those guaranteeing freedom of speech, press, assembly, and religion, and that no person be denied "equal protection of the laws"). Sometimes they give broader interpretations of those rights than does the U.S. Supreme Court.

California's Mixed Liberties And Rights Record: Denials

California's Supreme Court has often led the nation in protecting liberties and rights within its jurisdiction. And the California Legislature has enacted civil rights laws predating similar national legislation. Still, California's rights record is mixed.

In 1850, Indians and Negroes were forbidden by law to testify against Caucasians. In 1852, the California Supreme Court banned such testimony by Chinese. In 1860, Indians, Negroes and Mongolians were banned from California's public schools. In 1879, California's Constitution forbade employment of Chinese by corporations or on public works. In 1882, Chinese were excluded from migrating to the U.S. (largely because of pressure originating in California). In 1924, the ban was extended to all Asians. (It particularly targeted Japanese — as did the 1913 California Alien Land Law, which prohibited aliens ineligible for citizenship from owning land or leasing it for more than three years).

In the depression years of the 1930s, California attempted to bar indigent people, (principally poor whites) from Oklahoma and Arkansas — refugees from the dust bowl, and the federal government deported tens of thousands of Californians of Mexican ancestry, many of them American citizens. During World War II, resident Japanese (including those who were American citizens) were forced (by federal authority) into detention camps. (Leading the campaign for internment was California Attorney General Earl Warren). In 1989, former UC Chancellor Ira Heyman admitted to extensive hindering of Asian Americans in the admissions process at UC. In 1994, Proposition 187 made undocumented immigrants ineligible for public education and other state financed services, including medical care (except emergency health care).* In 1998, Proposition 207 was passed seeking to end bilingual education in public schools. Also in 1998, the state high court ruled that a single criminal act can count as more than one crime under the three-strikes law.

In 2006, modern day slavery is permitted in sweatshops in California. Prosecutions are almost exclusively of *sex sweatshops*. The reason: The government gets a great deal of favorable press coverage for prosecuting sex sweatshops. It could prosecute all non-sex sweatshops (the vast majority of sweatshops). But it does not.

California's Mixed Liberties And Rights Record: Extensions

But examples of extension of rights in California also abound. California's Constitution of 1849 incorporated the entire federal Bill of Rights, forbade slavery, protected a wife's separate property, granted suffrage to adult white male citizens, and authorized the Legislature to extend the vote to Indians. And California's current Constitution has a Declaration of Rights longer than the entire U.S. Constitution.

Furthermore, California's Legislature was the first state legislature to furnish financial indemnity to victims of violent crime. It was also in the vanguard in enacting open housing legislation. It extended the Unruh Civil Rights Act (1959) — which prohibited discrimination by businesses selling or leasing real estate — to cover certain residential housing, and enacted the 1963 Rumford Act, which prohibited discrimination in the sale or rental of most California real estate. (Rumford predated the federal Open Housing Law by half a decade). It passed Governor Jerry Brown's Farm Labor Act which gave enforceable rights for the first time to our most downtrodden workers. California's 1967 Lanterman-Petris-Short Act (significantly amended in 2000), preventing involuntary commitment of mentally disturbed persons not deemed dangerous to themselves, was a pioneering step in the nationwide transformation of mental health laws. California also pioneered in 1975, with its so-called Inmate Bill of Rights, which guaranteed prison inmates most of the civil rights and liberties of citizens. (The scope of the law was narrowed, however, by 1994 amendments, for instance, halting government financing of inmate lawsuits challenging prison regulations).

---

*Proposition 187 does *not* address border enforcement *or* prevention of the employment of undocumented immigrants. Its principal goal was to incite lawsuits which could result in overturning a 5-4 U.S. Supreme Court ruling *(Pyler v. Doe*, 1982) requiring states to educate undocumented immigrants. It was nullified by the courts (as unconstitutional).

César Chavez (1927-1993), a humble agricultural worker who by choice sustained a life of poverty, led in the 1960's, 1970's, and early 1980's, a movement of America's poorest of workers against the perennial exploitation of their labor by powerful land barons of the Southwest. It was a most unequal of contests. Yet he won.

Sacramento Bee/Dick Schmidt

But when Chavez thought to challenge the massive political-economic establishment of California in the state house, the courts, and the Agricultural Labor Relations Board, to make permanent the workers' gains and protect them (and consumers across the nation) from the birth defects and cancer many link to unregulated pesticide spraying, he and his movement were crushed.

The California courts have also pioneered the development of rights nationally. For example, in 1946 (**Mendez v. Westminster**), a federal court supported a California court in outlawing segregation of Latino students. In 1955, California's Supreme Court ruled **(People v. Caban)** evidence secured by police authorities in "unreasonable" searches not admissible in criminal trials. This was six years before **Mapp v. Ohio,** a landmark case in which the U.S. Supreme Court recognized this right. Later, in **People v. Dorado** (1965), the California Supreme Court decided that defendants must be apprised of their rights to an attorney. This was a year before the U.S. Supreme Court made this a national mandate in **Miranda v. Arizona.** In **Mulkey v. Reitman** (1966) the California Supreme Court invalidated an anti-fair fair housing initiative approved by the voters. In **Serrano v. Priest** (1977), it outlawed the method whereby California public schools were financed, ruling that it violated the "equal protection" clause of both the U.S. Constitution and the California Constitution because financing through the property tax discriminates against children living in poorer areas. It maintained its decision even after the U.S. Supreme Court stated that the U.S. Constitution said nothing concerning how public education is financed.

In 1992, Governor Wilson signed separate bills banning discrimination against gays and lesbians, and against people testing positive for the AIDS-causing HIV virus; in 1993, the Leonard Bill guaranteed "...that a student shall have the same right to exercise his or her right to free speech on campus as he or she enjoys when off campus;* in 1995, the UC Board of Regents required UC to stop using "race, religion, gender, color, ethnicity or national origin" as criteria in its admissions policies (and hiring and contracting practices); in 1996 the San Francisco Board of Education eliminated a requirement at Lowell High School that Chinese American students must score higher on admission exams than must other racial and ethnic groups. In 2000, Governor Davis signed a bill to make March 31, César Chávez's birthday, a paid state holiday for state workers — the first such state holiday to honor a Latino or an organized labor leader. That same year, the Governor approved legislation which, among other things, extended civil rights protection to gays and lesbians in the areas of housing and jobs, and guaranteed their right to serve on juries. In 2001, a law was passed which granted in-state tuition to undocumented students who attended California high schools for three years and graduated. In 2002 and 2003, the Governor signed bills providing rights married couples possess to gay, lesbian, and senior partners. In 2003, Governor Davis signed legislation, authored by Senator Gil Cedillo, which would permit undocumented aliens to get driver's licenses. He had vetoed two such bills.**. In that year he also signed a bill that provided California the strictest financial privacy laws in the nation. In 2003, he furthermore signed domestic partners legislation, which gives same-sex couples expanded rights. In 2005, Governor Schwarzenegger began emphasizing rehabilitation of imprisoned felons (instead of punishment), this hopefully to reverse a recidivism rate that is currently the highest in the nation. Also in 2005, he vetoed legislation providing for same-sex marriages. He cited an initiative constitutional amendment (Prop. 22), approved by the voters in 2000, which forbid marriage between couples of the same gender.

In 2006, he signed a bill which added sexual orientation to the state's nondiscrimination statutes. But that year he vetoed legislation that would have permitted illegal entrants to obtain financial aid for college.

In 2008, he signed a measure banning texting while driving (sending, writing, or reading text messages), effective January 1, 2009. Driving while holding a cellphone had previously been banned.

In 2008, the voters approved Proposition 8, a constitutional amendment which eliminated the right of same-sex couples to marry.

*The law applies to secondary schools, colleges, and universities, and was the first if its kind in the U.S.

**Governor Schwarzenegger got the law voided.

4 CHAPTER

Demographic, Economic, Geographic and National Aspects

Demographic Aspects

California's population has grown enormously since 1981, up from about 23,500,000 to about 38,000,000 in 2008. It is the most populous and fastest growing American state. Accounting for much of this boom are immigrants, about five-sixths coming from other nations, and most of these from Central America, Mexico, and from Asian countries of the Pacific Rim, a tide which has made already immigrant-rich California the most racially and culturally diverse society in the world.

Within this decade, Latinos will outnumber non-Latino whites in California. Today, whites (non-Latino) constitute only about 47 percent of the California population, Asians about 13 percent, blacks about 7 percent, Native Americans, Aleuts, and Eskimos about 6. The US. Census Bureau reports that 43 percent of Californians and 53 percent of the residents of Los Angeles speak a language other than English in their private lives.

Whites (non-Latino) are also substantially older (median age is 40.3) than are ethnics, relatively affluent, and likely to be home owners. Ethnics domain of its white (non-Latino) population, with election campaigns primarily directed at an electorate that is mainly white middle class. The reason is simple: while whites constitute less than 50 percent of the state's population, they are nearly 72 percent of California voters.

Whites (non-Latino) are also substantially older (median age is 40.3) than are ethnics, relatively affluent, and likely to be home owners. Ethnics are young (median age of Latinos is under 24), relatively poor (Latinos are now the poorest minority.), likely to be renters, have a high birth rate, and by their numbers particularly burgeon requirements for schools, jobs, housing, roads, pollution control and other environmental protection. California also has the highest youth population of any state, and the most elderly (requiring eldercare).

The result is obvious: a California politics that is increasingly ethnic, class, and generation based. And as the age gap widens and the youthful nonwhite population continues to explode, it seems our apparently perennial problem — the underlying social struggle between those who have and those who have not — will greatly govern California's politics.

The Impact of Geography

California is immense, stretching some 1264 miles along the Pacific coastline from the Mexican border northward to Oregon and extending 150 to 375 miles inland to neighboring Arizona and Nevada. It is bigger than England, Italy, Japan, or Poland, and save Alaska and Texas larger than any other American state. And it is advantageously located — at the juncture of North America, Latin America, and the Pacific Rim — to seize upon burgeoning international markets.

California also has the most imposing mountain range in the U.S. — the Sierra Nevada. Extending down almost two thirds of the eastern borderlands of the state, if not only supplies most of California's water, but merging with the Coast Ranges on the west encloses its great Central Valley, the richest agricultural heartland of the U.S, (and perhaps the world), and yet another phenomenon of California — a great agricultural empire in the most urbanized American state (Figure 1).

And California's lowland coastal strip, delightfully cooled by marine breezes and stretching from the Mexican border to a few miles north of San Francisco, is home to most Californians. But, fastest growing areas are mostly inland, where the summers are hot but housing is more affordable, and in the inner cities, which are attracting foreign immigrants with limited skills. Near future boom areas — in both absolute numbers and rate of growth — should also be in the interior, in the "Inland Empire" (Riverside and San Bernardino Counties), the San Joaquin Valley, the eleven-county Sacramento area, and parts of San Diego County.

California's geography also greatly impacted its politics in other ways. The North (north of the Tehachapi Mountains) is heavily forested and relatively wet, while the South is arid. Thus, North versus South rivalry was historically endemic, and principally over water distribution (and allocation of tax funds), it was also ideological and partisan, Northern Californians tended toward liberalism and the Democratic Party, and Southern Californians toward conservatism and the Republican Party. In more recent years, interior against coastal areas rivalry often exceeded North versus South.

By 2000, the partisan split was distinctly between coastal and inland, with Democrats (for instance, strongly backing environmental measures) dominant in the coastal areas, and Republicans (for instance, strongly backing conservative stands on social issues) dominant in inland areas.

This coastal versus inland rivalry is over such things as freeway improvements, rail financing, expansion of air hubs, affordable housing, and land use. Geography similarly figures in rivalries between big cities and suburbs, and between rural and urban interests (increasingly over water distribution), and between both real estate developers and extractive industries and conservationists (e.g., over uses of the state's vast shoreline, great interior deserts, and mountain wildernesses).

Figure 1. California Land Forms

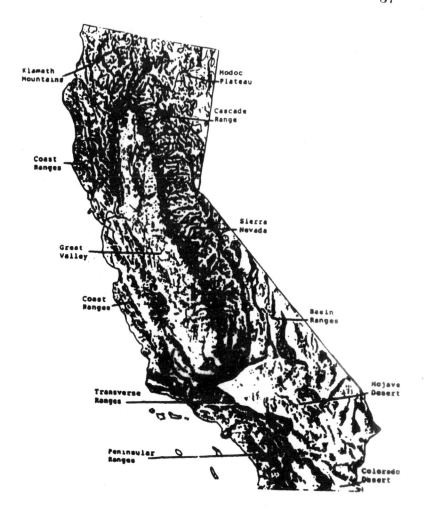

California's Changing Economy

Today, Californias economy is the eighth largest economy in the world. Among American states it is by far the largest exporter, foremost in agriculture, aerospace, the defense industry, commercial fishing, and pop culture; second in over-all manufacturing and in commercial timber production; third in oil and mineral output; has a bustling construction industry; and is home to much of the communications industry (movies, TV, records)*. Its great seaports (principally San Francisco, Los Angeles, and San Diego) host enormous naval facilities and accommodate one-seventh of the nation's exports. Los Angeles is the nation's largest commercial seaport, Long Beach is the second largest. Their importance may be relatively diminished when Panama widens the Panama Canal, which is planned and financed. Not surprisingly, these leading industries are major players in California politics.

*Currently, more Southern Californians work in multimedia than in aerospace.

THE CALIFORNIA INCOME GAP

Twenty years ago California was not a poverty state. But currently (according to the U.S. Census Bureau), the poverty rate of California is higher than the national percent, and the gap between the rich and poor continues to increase, rising faster than in the nation as a whole. Also, despite the end of the national recession in 1991, California's unemployment remains above the national average. Furthermore, most jobs created in the past six years have been poverty level. Gone are the lush days of post World War II. When California per capita income was approximately one third more than the rest of the U.S. Since the 1990's, per capita income in California has been about equal to the national average. Furthermore the incidents of poverty are rising acutely in California, particularly among Latinos and African-Americans.

Fortunately, there are ways other than economic prosperity, though, to lift up the disadvantaged. Certain educational programs (i.e., the Cal-Grant program), more welfare reform, increase of the minimum wage,* improvement in the climate of union organization, and more low-income housing would narrow the gap.

Though California's economy has produced more millionaires than has any other state's economy, not all Californians share the wealth. There is a startling level of economic inequality in the state. Actually, California leads the nation in income inequality.

Still stressing the economy are huge budget deficits, high power costs, a state government in need of major reconstruction, high housing and insurance costs, an economic environment that often repels business and jobs, troubled schools, traffic congestion, chronic water shortages, and the smog which still blunts California's climactic advantage. Also, the states portion of military - related spending has declined from 23 percent in the 1980s to 15 percent today. Moreover, state finances have been in some disarray since the enactment in 1978 of Proposition 13 — the renowned property tax reduction initiative which has eviscerated local government finances and induced a reallotment of state revenues.

*The minimum wage in California was in late 2006, raised from $6.75 to $8.00 per hour. Minimum wage earners got a 75 cent increase on January 1, 2007. They will get an additional 50 cents in January 1, 2008.

Yet, many of the Golden State's traditional advantages obtain. Tax rates, which were among the nation's highest, drifted in recent years to near the national average. The national appetite for California goods and services remains high. California exports have actually grown by more than 80 percent since 1988. And the Department of Finance indicates that California has gained substantially from the Common Market linking the U.S., Mexico, and Canada. But there is no guarantee, that any "gains" California experiences will be distributed equitably.

California's Political Prominence and National Trendsetting

California is notably prominent in the American political system. It has more votes in the national party nominating conventions than does any other state. Also, California has 55 presidential electoral votes, 21 more than the second most populous state, Texas. All of this greatly advantages California's politicians (and particularly its Governors). In 1960, 1968, 1972, 1980, and 1984, a Californian won nomination for President, and four times Californians have been elected President (Richard Nixon in 1968 and 1972, and Ronald Reagan in 1980 and 1984).

California also leads all states in numbers of representatives in Congress. It was assigned 53 seats in the U.S. House by the 2002 congressional reapportionment But historically disjuncted by distinctions entailing geography and ideology, California's delegation has seldom been in agreement. Furthermore, it continues to face antagonism from other state delegations apprehensive over California's political "dominance". This opposition is completely groundless. While California's voting power in the U.S. House is based quite accurately on its current population relative to that of the other states, California is grotesquely underrepresented in the U.S. Senate. For instance, with a population of 34,501,000 in the 2000 census, it has the same vote in the Senate (2) as Wyoming, with a population of 494,000. It takes about 69 California votes to equal one Wyoming vote. Whether it is a vote on a bill, organization of the Senate, a treaty, a major federal appointment, or a proposal of a constitutional amendment, California voters are at distinct disadvantage. California is the most unrepresented state. Understandably, it is not expected that any small state will relinquish its equal representation in the Senate specifically guaranteed it in the U.S. Constitution. But California is not legitimately faulted for being "politically dominant."

Diane Feinstein (D)   Barbara Boxer (D)

United States Senators

California's political prominence also derives from its trend setting. Californians are disposed to try the new and different to solve problems, efforts which get national attention — and frequent emulation. Initiative, referendum, and recall provisions of the California Constitution have made their way into many state Constitutions. California was the first state to pass a stiff clean water initiative (Proposition 65) and mandate clean air rules, and ideas relating to California's Proposition 13 (the property tax initiative) and its "three-strikes" legislation overspread much of the nation. Also, Proposition 187 focused national attention on immigration,   as Proposition 209 did on race-and gender based affirmative action. Popular approval of term limits on California state legislators and on most other state constitutional officers in 1990 (and the California Supreme Court's decision validating these limits), boosted the term-limit movement nation-wide. And Proposition 227 (1998), requiring public school instruction in English only may influence other states, and California legislation (2002) limiting global warming (especially limiting greenhouse gases from vehicles), permitting some stem cell research, paid family leave, and privacy legislation protecting against identity theft will likely be emulated by other states.

EDUCATIONAL AIDS FOR STUDENTS IN CALIFORNIA: 8.1 BILLION

FFEL & FDSL Programs	50.53%	$4,099,623,000
Federal Pell Grants *	16.17%	$1,312,312,000
Other Federal Aid	1.71%	$139,005,000
Federal Work-Study	1.43%	$115,629,000
Federal Perkins Loans	0.95%	$77,396,000
Cal Grants	**6.72%**	**$544,900,000**
Other State Aid	**2.89%**	**$234,343,000**
State Work-Study	**0.06%**	**$4,662,000**
Institutional Aid	18.05%	$1,464,804,000
Other Aid	1.49%	$120,995,000

*In 2009, Pell Grants were raised to over $5000 per year to each recipient.

CAL-GRANT PROGRAM

In 1960, California promised college access for all students with good grades, but the state never had enough money to cover all eligible. In 2000, however, Governor Davis signed a bill creating the Cal-Grant program providing scholarships for all needy students who have a C average or better.

> # FUNDED BY THE STATE OF CALIFORNIA AND ADMINISTERED BY THE <u>CALIFORNIA STUDENT AID COMMISSION</u>, CAL GRANTS ARE ONE OF THE SMARTEST WAYS TO GET CASH FOR COLLEGE.

ABOUT CAL GRANTS OVERVIEW

NEED CASH FOR COLLEGE? YOU COULD GET A CAL GRANT.

Cal Grants are one of the smartest ways to get cash for college. For starters, it's money you don't have to pay back. And secondly, it's guaranteed. If you're a graduating high school senior or recent graduate, meet academic, financial and eligibility requirements and submit two forms by March 2, you are guaranteed a Cal Grant!

How Much Money Are We Talking About?

With a Cal Grant you can get up to $9,700 a year to pay for college expenses at any qualifying California college, university or career or technical school in California. Depending on <u>which Cal Grant you get</u>, the money can be used for tuition, room and board, even books and pencils. The best part is, it's yours to keep and you don't have to pay it back.

Here's How to Get It.

All you have to do is submit the FAFSA (Free Application for Federal Student Aid) between January 1 and March 2 and submit a verified Cal Grant GPA anytime between November and the March 2 deadline. If you meet the income, eligibility, and GPA requirements, the cash is yours. The best part is, you can fill out the FAFSA online.

To submit a verified Cal Grant GPA, first check with your school to see if they will do it for you. If not, you can go online and download a GPA Verification form, fill out the student section and take it to your school. Don't let a little paperwork stand between you and a Cal Grant.

> # CAL GRANTS MAY BE USED AT ANY <u>CALIFORNIA COMMUNITY COLLEGE, UCS, CSUS, PRIVATE AND MOST CAREER/TECHNICAL SCHOOLS.</u>

If you are interested, see a college counselor.

THE INFRASTRUCTURE

In the 1950s and 1960s, California spent 15% to 20% of the general fund on the infrastructure. Its universities, water projects, roads and parks were the envy of other states. But for the last four or five decades, California governors and legislators have permitted our state's infrastructure to deteriorate. This reflected to a considerable extent deliberate choices that favor immediate considerations rather than long-term investments.

A series of exceptions was Governor Davis' award of over $5 billion for transportation and $15 billion for public schools. He also began a major expansion of college scholarships. These outlays were possible because of a $14 billion surplus in the 2000-2001 state budget

Governor Schwarzenegger designated 2006 as a year of rebuilding, with specific emphasis on the state's infrastructure. In the 2006 gubernatorial election all five infrastructure bonds (total, about $43 billion) passed. This time the voters had confidence to vote yes because the issues had been approved by two thirds of the the legislators, and by the Governor.

Since Governor Schwarzenegger took office, California has had a bonded indebtedness of about $45 billion. Even with the current low rate of interest, the interest on the indebtedness will cost about $3 billion a year.

THE ENVIRONMENT

Federal legislation, beginning in the early 1970's, shoved the environment onto the California agenda. The federal government set the national standards of water and air quality, passed a toxic substance act, created the Environmental Protection Agency, and required environmental impact statements of the effects of new developments on the environment. It left to the states responsibility for executing standards and enforcing compliance.

California, in addition to seeing to implementation of federal criteria, lead the way in areas such as water and sewage services, recycling, preservation, and waste management. It established its own Environmental Quality Act.

In 2006, Governor Schwarzenegger signed a law that requires that 20% of California's electricity must come from renewable sources by 2010, and 33% by 2020.* Coal burning power plants cause over 40% of the nation's carbon dioxide, which causes global warming.

In 2006, he signed an antiglobal warming bill that became the nation's first cap on greenhouse emissions. It was designed to reduce greenhouse gases by about 25% by 2020.

California regulations require motor vehicles to average 36 M.P.G. by 2016.

In 2008, California's Air Resources Board capped about every segment of the economy. Thus far this is more coverage than any other state. But possibly California's most pressing problem at present is the question of the collection and distribution of water.

*Wind and sunshine are currently the most promising renewable resource

5 CHAPTER

CALIFORNIA'S FINANCIAL POLICIES

Governor Davis' Last Budget

After winning reelection in 2002, Governor Davis, in early 2003, at first sought to do what Governor Wilson did wih the $14.3 billion gap in the 1991-1992 budget, raise taxes and cut programs. But Democratic and Republican legislators resisted. Democrats did not want deep budget cuts. Republicans were firm in voting against any new taxes and refusing to give up previous tax cuts.

Republicans had enough votes to negate the Constitution's 2/3 majority needed to enact a state budget. Democrats in the end caved in to Republicans' "no new taxes" demand. Davis, by now facing a recall and needing a completed budget to retain his base in the Democratic party, agreed to sign the 2003-2004 budget, with its $38 billion deficit. In August, 2003, Californina had the lowest credit rating in all 50 American states. Davis was recalled in 2003.

Five Proposed Remedies to California's Fiscal Dysfunction

Recalling a governor will not solve California's fiscal crisis. And we are not going to recall legislators or Supreme Court justices. Suggested reforms, though, directed at clearing up the crises are legion. Five of the most prominent are these:

A "RAINY DAY" FUND *

1. Faced with a $14.5 billion shortfall in his 2008-2009 budget, Governor Schwarzenegger proposed his idea of an amendment to the state constitution to mandate retention of a portion of the surplus in good revenue years to avoid cuts in services, tax increases, or borrowing in bad revenue years.

Both Governors Gray Davis and Pete Wilson supported the idea of establishing a "rainy day" fund.

PROVIDING FOR NONPARTISAN REDISTRICTING

2. The circumstances which made the sometimes benign 2/3 rule a catastrophe this time was the *partisan reapportionment* of the Legislature in 2001. This reapportionment, making nearly all seats safely Democratic or safely Republican, virtually eliminated two-party competition, made nearly all incumbents impervious to constituent pressure, and reduced the number of compromised-minded moderates.

*In 2004, the voters did approve Proposition 58, which provided for a "rainy day" fund, But the fund idea does not work when (as in recent years) nearly every year is a "rainy day" (more spent than revenues taken in).

Proposition 11, an amendment approved by the voters in 2008, transfers the power to set state legislative boundaries from the legislature to an elected commission. This could result in more competitive races in 2010.

3. ENDING OR REDUCING TERM LIMITS

In 1990, *term limits* on legislators were constitutionally mandated by the voters to rid the Legislature of careerist politicians. The measure limited members to six years in the Assembly and eight years in the Senate. Governor Schwarzeneggar in 2009, favored extending term limits.

Many of those creating the fiscal catastrophe were among the state's most experienced politicians. Many senators had served as legislators over 10 years. Senate President *pro tem* John Burton had served in the Legislature for about 25 years. Governor Davis probably was more experienced in elective office than almost any governor.* Chief Justice Ronald George had been on the Supreme Court about 12 years.

In 2008, the voters again rejected a change in term limits, thus the Speaker of the Assembly (Fabian Nuñez), and the President Pro Tem of the Senate (Don Perata) were termed out.

4. ELIMINATING THE 2/3 RULE TO PASSAGE OF A BUDGET

The 2/3 rule has been in the California Constitution for more than 75 years. The fact that it can be overcome has been demonstrated many times. A legislature in a truly bipartisan mode can do so. But unfortunately in recent years, it is often overcome with bipartisan collusion. With the latter design, Democrats have gotten Republican legislators' support for the budget by offering them billions of dollars in tax cuts and spending large amounts of money in their districts.

Some say that without the 2/3 rule we would have excessive spending. But with the 2/3 rule we had over a 40% increase in spending in the past eight years. In 2009, the Governor proposed a 5% limit on tax increases, along with abolishing the 2/3 rule (and proposing a vote less than 2/3).

The year of 2009 may be the year in which Californians resolve that their political structure is broken, and that particularly their system of writing our deficit-burdened budgets must be changed. The 2009-2010 budget, with its about $40 billion deficit, had new cuts and taxes which hurt the middle class and the poor.

*He served as chief of staff to a Governor. He was elected an Assemblyman in 1982, Controller in 1986 and in 1990, Lieutenant Governor in 1994, and Governor in 1998 and 2002.

Proposition 13, the renowned property tax limitation initiative (see box), approved by the voters in 1978, remains probably the defining issue of California politics. The reason is this: It meant revenue loss, which, coincident with California's population explosion, left the state's governments unable to fund the level of services that law and popular claims indicate. Especially hard hit were counties, cities, and school and other special districts, which depended on local property taxes. Confronted with monstrous revenue shortfalls they turned to Sacramento for operating funds, thus increasing state fiscal responsibility — and control.

There was justification for Proposition 13. Tax assessments, because of massive inflation in real estate values, had doubled and tripled in the 1970's.

But Prop. 13 created inequities, which with time deepened. Some California homeowners pay several times as much as neighbors who owned similar homes prior to Prop. 13, and start-up businesses pay two or three times higher property taxes than their established competitors. Moreover, most of the tax relief goes not to homeowners, but to commercial and income property. Business property is currently reassessed less often than houses because it changes ownership less often.

PROPOSITION 13
(PROPERTY TAX INITIATIVE)

1. Rolled back one's property tax bill to *one percent of the property value on March 1, 1975*, with annual inflation adjustment of no more than two percent as long as the property remains under the same ownership.

2. Provided that the rate of taxation be increased only when the property is sold, at which time the increase is to *one percent of its current market value* on the change of ownersh'   :te.

3. Barred new property taxes.

4. Prohibited local governments from imp sing other new taxes without a two-thirds vote of local voters. (Except that since 2000, certain school bonds require only 55% vote of local voters.).

That these inequities may be effectively addressed while also cushioning homeowners from big tax increases has been widely recognized. But these tidings will almost certainly be lost on the voters, two thirds of whom are homeowners. Most oppose any tampering with the Proposition. It has become to them a symbol of social stratification and a defense of their economic security, which they feel is menaced by government, as well as by a mushrooming nonhomeowning and largely nonwhite population needing government services.

In 1992, the U.S. Supreme Court called Proposition 13

"distasteful and unwise," but nevertheless upheld its constitutionality in an 8-1 ruling. Furthermore, the California Legislature is not likely to void the popular Proposition soon, and levy higher property taxes. The political climate is no more conducive to increasing property taxes now than it was more than 30 years ago.

THE STATE BUDGET PROCESS

The California Budget is more than simply a fiscal document. It generally drives state policy, and its creation is the Governor's main legal responsibility. The governor has at the beginning the authority to draft a budget and at the end the item veto. It is also the legislator's most significant responsibility. The voters, through use of initiative and referendum, also have an important role.

California's Governor, unlike the President, must set out to achieve a balanced budget. But the California constitution does not require the budget *passed* by the Legislature be balanced.

Early in the budget process, the Governor outlines his budget policy. Then, state agencies make their budgetary requests, which are reviewed by the Department of Finance, acting on the Governor's behalf. In early January, he proffers to the Legislature his budget proposal, which projects both state revenues and expenditures for the fiscal year commencing July 1. His proposal is analyzed by the nonpartisan Legislative Analyst and studied by the Finance Committees in the two houses.

Differences between the houses on the Governor's proposals are reconciled in a conference committee composed of three Assembly and three Senate members. When finally considered by the Legislature, a two-thirds vote in both houses is needed for passage, a constitutional mandate that gives the minority party (or a coalition) potential power to block the budget. The Constitution requires the Legislature to approve a budget by June 15. But the deadline has seldom been met.

State Revenues and Expenditures

California state government gets its money from taxes, fees, bond sales, and from other levels of government. Almost 85 percent comes from the state personal income tax, sales and use taxes, bank and corporation taxes and motor vehicle fees.

The primary recipient is K through 12 education, which was guaranteed top spending priority by Proposition 98 (passed in 1988). Next are health and human services, a reflection of the reduced ability of local governments to raise money for education, health, and welfare through property taxes since Proposition 13.

As much as 70 percent of the expenditures in California budgets are mandated by voter initiatives, laws, or court orders,

6 CHAPTER

California's Strong Pressure Groups, Weak Parties, and Elections

CALIFORNIA PRESSURE GROUPS

California's pressure groups, unlike California's parties are strong, and their impact is increasing. They employ nearly 2000 lobbyists, many of whom have several clients.

Like their national counterparts, lobbyists for California pressure groups seek to influence legislatures (particularly their leaders), the executives (including bureaucrats), and the courts (especially by bringing court cases). They target the voters through TV and newspapers.

Lobbyists propose most bills introduced in the Legislature, fashion legislative stratagems, often manipulate the media, lobby on the local level, and increasingly become more powerful through use of the initiative process. They are also both sources and conduits for political contributions. The biggest spenders by far are large corporate pressure groups, all of which are represented by lobbyists in Sacramento.

With their extensive client lists and huge staffs, pressure groups are increasingly dominant. The struggle is now familiar: the concentrated power of special interests versus the largely unfocused, unrepresented, and uninformed public interest, an increasingly uneven contest.

About the current role in California government of pressure groups, Dan Walters and Jay Michael assert that "...the public face of politics — the campaigns ..., the legislative hearings, the debates on bills, the news conferences and media events — are just for show, and that lobbyists represent the real focus of the Capitol that most of the public don't even know exists."*

Arizona and Maine have systems which feature nearly 100% public financing of elections and low spending limitations. In California a similar plan may be proposed in initiative form for the 2006 ballot. Cost to California taxpayers of public financing would be about $7 a year for each eligible voter. The proposal is based on the reasoning that if the voters do not control the politicians, the special interests will.

Though business lobbies' expenditures are paramount, many organizations with strong "grass roots," for instance, "people's lobbies" such as Common Cause and the League of Women Voters, play important parts, as do issue, occupational, and various other nonbusiness groups. Instead of using money, these groups typically provide campaign volunteers to operate phone banks and ask for support in personal interviews. In any event, pressure group activity is protected by the U.S. Constitution's guarantee of freedom to petition government.

*Dan Walters and Jay Michael , *The Third House, California Journal*, 2002. Walters is a veteran columnist and Jay Michael is a long time lobbyist.

With term limits in full sway, the influence of lobbyists is further inflated. The reasons are these: compared to the most influential lobbyists, California Assembly members restricted to six years in office, and Senators restricted to eight, possess less experience. This condition has worsened as term-limited ex-legislators have become lobbyists. A new term-limited legislator, for instance, who enters office distrusting lobbyists and resists trafficking with them still must engage in fund-raising (for reelection campaigns) — the main interaction between legislators and lobbyists. Also term limited leaders lack the clout they had previously to maintain order and deal with the executive branch and vested interests. Thus they are partially negated by term limits.

Finally, with term limits increasing the number of legislative races without an incumbent, special interest lobbies, in a sharp departure from past practices, have become heavily involved in financing *primary election campaigns.*

Regulation Of Pressure Groups

Lobbyists' activities in California are regulated by a 1974 reform initiative, **Proposition** 9. They must register with the Secretary of State, and both they and their employers must file public financial reports. Those not reporting face cease and desist orders or fines by the Fair Political Practices Commission, and some bad press. **Proposition** 9 has not reduced spending by pressure groups, but clearly the amount spent on legislators (limited to $10 per month per legislator) for meals and liquor is less. Other than that, and the inconvenience of reporting, lobbyists seem little hindered by the act.

A 1990 referendum (**Proposition** 112) prohibited members of the Legislature from accepting speaking fees. This law, however, left lobbyists many other ways to contribute to legislators, including, but not limited to, campaign contributions. They also can still spend on ballot issues, and on local lobbying.

One consideration that may help, although perhaps not very much, is **Proposition** 39, passed in 2000. This Proposition bans lobbyists from contributing directly to the campaigns of officials they lobby. But the proposition has been rather easily evaded. It simply makes special interests adopt different ways to finance their candidates. A favorite scheme of the special interests is to contribute to independent expenditure committees. These committees (following court rulings) are not limited.

To control lobbyists better we could pass disclosure laws to show which lobby or lobbies is paying to pass or kill laws (or effect their administration), and how nearly this spending by lobbyists interrelates with voting records and other behavior of elected officers.

PARTY AFTER THE TURN OF THE CENTURY

California's two major parties, like their national counterparts, have been weak. In California, this is by design (dating from the progressive era) and is due principally to: (1) nonpartisan local, school, and judicial elections, (2) parties with little patronage, nearly all state government jobs being covered by the civil service merit system, (3) bipartisanship, (4) cross-filing,* and (5) tradition.

Though California parties have a long practice of bipartisanship and progressivism, the parties are currently in a state of political extremism and gridlock. Probably the major reason for the current morass is the partisan redistricting of the legislature after the 2000 census. It created more partisanship by establishing "safe" districts for legislators (safely Democratic or safely Republican). With "safe" districts legislators need not reach out to new voters and other constituencies. Their base in the party is nearly all that matters to them. Ideological purity, not negotiation, is their insurance to endure in the legislature.

Currently, Democrats occupy the offices of Leiutenant Governor, all elective statewide executive offices, except Insurance Commisioner, and about two thirds of the seats in the Legislature. Registered Democrats outnumber registered Republicans by about 44% to 33%. The number of independents has been growing in recent years. They definitely tilt toward Democrats. Republicans are relatively conservative. Some of the things California Democrats tend to support: social programs, environmental betterment, health care, business regulation, most unions, affirmative action, gay marriage, gun control, and the liberal pro-choice positions on abortion rights. California Republicans favor law enforcement, incarceration, defense related matters, immigration control, and gun owners' rights. They oppose what they consider excess taxation. They are against affirmative action and gay marriage. They are pro-life on abortion.

Both parties present themselves as benefactors of public education. Neither wants to spend enough on the infrastructure. Most voters want more services but not more taxes.

Among ethnic groups, blacks vote about 9-1 Democratic. Whites are almost evenly divided between the major parties. Latinos and Asians vote about 2-1 Democratic. Young people, women, the middle aged, and older people all favor the Democrats, older people the least. Wealthy people vote Republican, the poor, Democratic, as does the middle class.

Californians are abandoning the major parties. Nearly 20 percent now identify as other than Democrat or Republican. Also, party labels, and "coattails" are diminishing as factors. Given these trends, voting could become yet more influenced by political advertising, personality, pressure groups, and short-term factors.

California's minor parties are even weaker. Having little chance to achieve power or even to effect the struggle between the major parties (though a minor party *may* take votes away from a major party candidate and thus affect the outcome of an election). The major parties cooperate on election laws to keep the minor parties weak.

* Cross-filing is an outdated practice whereby candidates could file in the opposition party primary as well as their own.

Informal Factional Organizations
within the Parties

The vacuum resulting from weak formal party organization is partially filled in California by informal volunteer organizations (and much more by pressure groups). Most prominent of the informal organizations within the parties have been the California Republican Assembly (CRA) and the California Democratic Council (CDC). The CRA and the CDC were particularly effective in the 1940's and 1950's. In recent elections their effectiveness has diminished because of rivalry from other volunteer groups and automation of campaigns, which has lessened the need for volunteer help. A fast growing organization is the California Republican League.

Party Structure and Functions

Parties may determine their organizational structure. Each has a biennial state party convention, a state central committee, and county central committees. The *state convention* drafts a party platform and selects its slate of presidential elector candidates. The *state central committee* chooses a state chairperson and an executive committee, musters financial support and otherwise helps party candidates. (But it is too big to operate very effectively.). *County committees* — with members elected by voting party adherents — raise money, register voters, and aid candidates for the Legislature as well as the U.S. House.

Contact between California's parties and their national counterparts is limited. It is principally through California's national committee members.

ELECTIONS

The State Primary System*

Beginning in 2002, a new legislatively created *Modified Closed Primary* provided that if you are registered to vote, *you may vote only for candidates from the party with which you are registered.* If you failed to select a political party when you registered to vote, *political parties may allow you to vote for their candidates anyway.* As previously, those candidates getting the greatest vote among their party colleagues would be on the general election ballot.

Since the redistricting after the 2000 Census made nearly all the California legislative and U.S. House districts essentially Democratic or Republican, the real contest is in the Primaries. Here party organizations *do not* choose their own office candidates. The voters do. But since candidates appeal to the extremes in their party's base the primaries produce conservative Republican legislators and liberal democratic legislators with next to none in the middle.

As before, all voters may vote on all ballot issues and for candidates for all nonpartisan offices.

In 2009, the Governor proposed a return to the open primary. He thought it would likely produce less extreme legislators.

---

*In 2007, the primary was moved to February 5th, hopefully to increase California's importance nationally. p. 48

The General Election

The general election is held on the first Tuesday after the first Monday in November of even numbered years. Voters choose between candidates for partisan offices nominated in the primary, between candidates in run-off elections to nonpartisan offices, for judicial offices, and for or against ballot propositions. In presidential election years, they also vote for California presidential electors, electors of the party getting the highest vote being elected.

Campaigns

In 1911, the Progressives transferred the focus of political campaigns from political parties to candidates and direct legislation. This has given scope to voters, but it also afforded opportunity to powerful personalities and pressure groups, with the result that expert media-oriented and strong financed campaigns and personal appeals are more significant than party.

To make up for organizational shortcomings of the parties, party candidates appoint consultants and management firms to sample voter opinion, fund raise, enlist campaign workers, advertise, and engage in numerous other campaign functions. Television, direct mail, radio, sophisticated databases, blogs, and the Internet predominate,   these being the best way to touch voters. Increasingly, the Internet is used to secure campaign contributions. In statewide contests, by far the most money is spent on TV ads. Most effective apparently are the negative ads which tend to demonize the opponent. All candidates now post web sites to give "information" and use email to correspond with followers and the media.

Restrictions enacted in 2000, limit the amount of contributions candidates can take for their election campaigns to state offices. But oversight is so underfinanced that the law is very weakly enforced.

There are no limits at all on funds raised for or against propositions on the ballot, making proponents more dependent on special interests.

Large contributors say their donations get them *access*. Politicians agree. Experience and common sense indicate, however, that there is more than access that their money gets them.

The 2003 Recall Election

Democratic Governor Gray Davis consistently received poor public approval ratings. They plummeted during the 2001 energy crisis and never recovered. He seldom pushed policy initiatives and permitted the Legislature to set the state's agenda. He did not reveal his $38 billion budget deficit until after his 2002 election victory. Davis endorsed unpopular programs such as drivers' licenses for undocumented, and an increase in the car owners' fees by up to 300%. At no time was he able to draw even in the recall election. He lost by 55% to 45%. Gray Davis was the first Governor to be recalled in California and only the second Governor to be recalled in the U.S.

About 30% of Democratic voters voted "yes" on the recall. Men voted strongly against Davis. Women were rather evenly divided. Union members and Latinos supported Davis, but not overwhelmingly. Black and Jewish voters were Davis' chief supporters.

Republican Arnold Schwarzenegger received about 49% of the votes cast for candidates to replace Governor Gray Davis (a winning plurality). He made a robust showing with a spectrum of voters. He got the votes of nearly 1/5 of Democratic voters, more than 40% of Independents' votes, and about 30% of the Latino vote.

Schwarzenegger ran a very disciplined campaign. He stuck to broad themes, thus avoiding alienating voters. He made these promises: to protect the people from special interests, have a fiscal overhaul, make California business friendly, help create jobs, cut motor vehicle taxes, and oppose drivers' licenses for undocumented. He promised not to raise taxes except for "an emergency." He challenged the political establishment saying often that "For the people to win, politics as usual must lose."

The 77 day recall campaign cost roughly the same amount per day as the past seven month gubernatorial campaign.

RECALL

California voters may remove any elected official. To recall an officer elected by a statewide vote, a petition containing signatures equal in number to at least twelve percent of all votes cast for all candidates for the involved office in the last election must be filed. To recall an official elected by a district of the state (e.g., state legislators or judges of the district courts of appeal), the petition must contain signatures of voters of the district equal to at least twenty percent of all votes cast for all candidates for the involved office at the last election.

The recall ballot states: "Shall (name of incumbent) be recalled ..." Those voting yes, or no, may then select from among other aspirants whose names are on the ballot. The ballot also contains a statement of charges, as well as a defense. (The incumbent need not have been charged with law violation.). If successful, he or she is reimbursed for election expenses, and is not subject to recall for at least six months.

In the 2006 gubernatorial election, Republican Governor Schwarzenegger was reelected by a landslide, getting a popular vote of about 63% to about 39% for Angelides. It was a victory for collaboration over confrontation. Schwarzenegger won largely because he abandoned confrontation with the Democrats in the Legislature for consensus.

Among his greatest achievements in his first term was a global warming measure (first in the U.S.), a raise in the minimum wage from $6.75 to $8.00, and about $43 billion in bond issues to furnish much needed infrastructure improvements. He also indicated that if reelected in 2006, health care would be his chief concern. Schwarzenegger spent about $27 million on the election, Angelides about $10 million.

> **Initiative and Referendum**
>
> In California, an initiated constitutional amendment requires a petition containing signatures of registered voters equal in number to eight percent of all votes cast for all candidates for Governor at the preceding gubernatorial election. For initiated statutes the formula is identical, except that the number of signatures required is only five percent. Initiated measures may deal with only one topic and are not subject to veto by the Governor.
>
> *Referendum* is used to block a state statute from going into effect. In California, any law except an urgency measure, or one calling an election, or one providing a tax levy or an appropriation for a usual state function may be blocked. A petition must be signed by voters equal in number to at least five percent of all votes cast for all candidates for Governor in the previous gubernatorial election. A qualified petition halts enforcement of the statute until the next general election when the voters choose to approve or reject it.
>
> State referendum is seldom used. The initiative has proved more workable.
>
> Initiative and referendum petitions may be proffered at primary and general elections, or at special elections called by the Governor. The state Legislature, other elected officials, organized interest groups, and private citizens use them.

Approval of both initiatives and referendums is by a majority of voters voting.

Statewide Initiative and Referendum

Hiram Johnson and the Progressives got the devices of initiative and referendum inserted into the California Constitution in 1911. They thought this first giving of legislative power to the voters would check gridlock and special interest dominated legislatures.

But today, **most** initiatives are sponsored by special interests or by politicians; and ballot issues are qualified through the efforts of hired professional petition businesses, not by volunteers. And there still is legislative gridlock and special interest domination.

While voters complain of numerous complicated and confusing issues on their ballots, well over 60 percent of them, feeling the initiative is still a powerful popular tool, support the device.

One of the few measures which passed in the 1990 general election limited the terms of state Senators and most statewide elected executives to two terms, and Assembly members to three (Proposition 140).

Three Strikes

Proposition 187

Proposition 184, the so-called "three strikes and you're out" initiative radically increased sentences for repeat felons. The law requires sentences of 25 years to life in prison when a defendant commits a third felony. Some district attorneys, however, do not always prosecute nonviolent offenses as three-strikes cases. Also, in 2001, voters approved Proposition 36, which substituted drug treatment for prison time for many defendants who would be subject under the three-strikes law. Proposition 187 (nullified by the courts as unconstitutional) made undocumented immigrants ineligible for public education and all other state-funded services (except emergency health care). Its principal goal was to incite lawsuits which could result in overturning a 5-4 U.S. Supreme Court ruling *(Pyler v. Doe*, 1982 *)* requiring states to educate undocumented immigrants.

The Open Primary

In the 1996 statewide primary, the voters endorsed only Proposition 198, the *Open Primary* Initiative. This statute allowed voters to traverse party lines in partisan primaries, thus giving the 12 percent of California voters registered as independents, and the increasing numbers registered as members of minor parties, an opportunity to participate in selecting the major parties' candidates. (The Proposition was declared unconstitutional by the U.S. Supreme Court in 2000.).

Affirmative Action
Marijuana for Medical Use

In the 1996 general election, California voters approved Proposition 209, which bars racial and gender preferences in government hiring, contracting, and education. (However, Proposition 209 could dispatch many programs endeavoring to assure racial equality.).

Also approved was Proposition 215, which permits use of marijuana for medical purposes (with a physician's recommendation).

English Instruction

Proposition 227 requires that all public school instruction be conducted in English, unless the child already knows English or would learn English faster through an alternative instruction technique.

School Property Tax Increases

Vouchers

Proposition 39 drops to 55 percent (from two-thirds) the requirement for enacting local school property tax increases. Rejected was Proposition 38, which would have established a voucher program through which parents would receive $4,000 per child from the state to pay tuition to a private school.

Before and After School Grants

Among the ballot issues, the voters approved Proposition 49 (before and after school grants) in the 2002 general election.
The proposition increased state spending by up to $455 million, beginning in 2004-2005. It provided that its program grants *not* be taken from education funds guaranteed by Proposition 98.

CALIFORNIA'S EXECUTIVE

CALIFORNIA'S EXECUTIVE

The influence of the Governor of California on the several issues Californians are now concerned about — for instance, *crime*, *immigration*, and *the economy* — is marginal. *Crime* principally reflects societal trends and demography. *Immigration* is a federal responsibility. *The economy* depends much more on the health of the national economy, federal spending, and the interest rate established as a result of Federal Reserve Board policies than on anything the Governor and legislators do. Furthermore, even in matters within the Governor's scope, legislators, lobbyists, and judges may frustrate his efforts.

Still, the Governor of California is probably second only to the President in political weight. His influence can be epic. He can animate the people of California to a compelling idea, cause, or plan which gets not only local, but also national and even international attention — and frequent emulation. Governor Hiram Johnson, for instance, ended the dominance of California by the Southern Pacific Railroad, secured the institution of the direct primary system of nomination, and the initiative process of popular legislation.

Governor Edmund G. (Pat) Brown pushed through a mammoth state water project, an extensive highway system, and a scheme of higher education — all part of an infrastructure which laid the base for years of economic prosperity in California.

Job of Being Governor of California

The job of being Governor of California is in many respects similar to the job of being President of the U.S. (yet another reason — in addition to his being the principal executive of the largest and most influential American state — that the Governor is invariably a potential candidate for President).

Both are expected to furnish executive and administrative leadership, see that the laws are faithfully executed, originate an annual budget, recommend legislation, veto "ill advised" bills, appoint top administrative and judicial officials, lead their party, perform ceremonial functions, exercise clemency, and serve as commander in chief of the military. Both are elected to four years terms*

* Prop. 140, November, 1990, so limits the Governor (and most elected state executives). Only one California Governor (Earl Warren) served more than two terms.

The Governor's role as chief of a non-sovereign state is more modest than the President's nationally. Still, he makes the most of this ceremonial role because it permits him to appear as a representative of all the people of the state and provides favorable contacts with constituents.

Chief of Party

Unlike governors of some smaller states, where a U.S. Senator, or a big city mayor may have more influence, or (his) party may be fragmented into local coteries more interested in local candidates, California's Governor (like the President) is the undoubted leader of his party.

Chief Legislator

California's Governor substantially influences the legislative product by his formal authority to (1) submit the state budget, (2) call the Legislature into special session (thus keeping legislators from ignoring his legislative program), (3) address the Legislature, (4) send messages recommending legislation and policies, (5) veto bills, and (6) use his item veto to strike out or reduce items of appropriations bills.

The Governor exercises the general veto several times as often as does the President, and while the Governor's vetoes (like the President's) may be overridden (by an absolute two-thirds vote of each legislative house), they rarely are.

Commander in Chief

The Governor heads the state militia (the National Guard), except when the President calls it into national service. Direct administration is by the Adjutant General, appointed by the Governor and approved by the President.

Generally, the Governor will use the Guard when state and local authorities cannot cope with situations, for instance, to quell riots or strikes, or deal with natural disasters such as fires, earthquakes, or floods. The Governor seldom calls on it unless requested by local authorities.

Judicial Officer

Like the President, the Governor, when making judicial appointments can substantially shape the judiciary in accordance with his views. Also like the President, he may grant clemency (pardons, reprieves, or commutations of sentences) to a person convicted of a felony. Though advised by the Adult Authority and the Board of Trustees of the California Institute for Women, the final decision is his (except he may not extend clemency in cases of impeachment, nor pardon a felon twice convicted of felonies except with approval of California's Supreme Court).

Chief Executive

Though the Governor's power of appointment is much less than the President's, his powers are substantial. He appoints (with the State Senate's approval) the Director of Finance, courts of appeal judges and Supreme Court Justices, the secretaries of principal administrative agencies, and about 100 members of various independent boards and commissions. He appoints his staff (in 2005, over 85 persons).

The Governor may also appoint U.S. Senators, state executive officers, and state judges, when vacancies occur because of disability, death, resignation, or conviction of crime. He may appoint to other state offices when no provision has been made for selection.

The Governor's Qualifications and Perquisites

The Governor must be a voter, a U.S. citizen, and five years a California resident. He is paid $212,179 per year in 2008,* gets an allowance for a rented home, an expense account for running his office, a chauffeured automobile, and a "contingency" expense allowance.

*Governor Schwarzenegger does not accept his salary.

The Lieutenant Governor

The Lieutenant Governor (John Garamendi, Democrat, elected 2006). He succeeds to the *office* of Governor should the Governor not be able to finish his term, exercises the *power* of Governor when the Governor is incapacitated or is absent from the state, and is a member of several state boards and commissions. He is President of the Senate and may vote to break a tie. While the President and Vice-President are always of the same party, this is not true of the Governor and Lieutenant Governor. He is elected separately from the Governor and is independent of him.

Other Elected Statewide Officials

The *Attorney General* (Jerry Brown, Democrat, elected 2006) is the head of the Justice Department, the state's chief law enforcement officer and legal advisor to state agencies, and after the Governor, the most important state executive. He gives advisory opinions on the constitutionality of state laws and local ordinances. The office is particularly attractive since it has proved a prime path to the governorship. Governors Edmund G. (Pat) Brown, Earl Warren, and George Deukmejian previously served as Attorney General.

The *Secretary of State* (Debra Bowen, Democrat, elected 2006). The Secretary of State is the state's elections officer and chief clerk, maintains the state's official records, accepts lobbyists' registrations and reports, and collects fees for incorporations.

The *Treasurer* (Bil Lockyer, Democrat, elected 2006) provides all custodial banking services for the state government and sees to the investment of securities.

The *Controller* (John Chiang, Democrat, elected 2006) is the state's chief disbursing and accounting official, administers a number of state taxes, and publishes statistics on local government.

The *Insurance Commissioner* (Steve Poizner, Republican, elected 2006) oversees the operations of the Department of Insurance and may approve or disapprove many kinds of insurance rates.

The *Superintendent of Public Instruction* (John O'Connell, elected 2002 and 2006), puts into force policies of the State Board of Education and is head of the Department of Education. The Superintendent is elected as a nonpartisan.

The **State Board of Equalization**, composed of the State Controller and four members elected by district, collects sales and other taxes, assesses the property of public utilities, and aids local assessors.

Managing the Bureaucracy

All executive departments except two (Justice and Education) are accountable to the Governor. Also, he may reorganize the administrative agencies (though subject to legislative veto). He is greatly assisted in managing the bureaucracy by the Department of Finance, which suggests fiscal policy, prepares the state budget, and oversees all financial activities of the state. Still, important boards and commissions are independent of him, and members' terms overlap his, thus diluting his appointment power. An example is the Public Utilities Commission.

The State Civil Service

California state employees, numbering more than 300,000 In 2008, are nearly all employed under the **merit system**. An aspect of California government employment since 1934, it features hiring and promotion on the basis of job skills, experience, and education, and protection from arbitrary dismissal and political pressure.

California's merit system has had some exceptions. **Collective bargaining agreements** set wages, benefits, and working conditions, and some work is **contracted out** to private employers who are not covered by the merit system. Furthermore, under **affirmative action** programs, historically underrepresented groups — e.g., blacks, Latinos, and women — have been hired and promoted over white males (classified as an "unprotected minority") who test higher, and during layoffs have been retained over white males with longer seniority. Latinos, Native Americans and the disabled are still underrepresented. (Latinos as a group are lowest paid.).

In June, 1995, Governor Pete Wilson, citing a series of U.S. Supreme Court rulings greatly checking the extent which race can be used as a factor in government state affirmative action programs. issued an executive order designed to dismantle affirmative action. In 1996, Proposition 209 eliminated state and local affirmative action programs.

8 CHAPTER

THE CALIFORNIA LEGISLATURE

Like Congress and the legislatures of all American states except Nebraska, California's legislature is bicameral (two houses). Its Assembly, the lower house, has 80 members elected for two-year terms, and its Senate, the upper house, has 40 members elected for four-year terms. All are selected in even numbered years, except that vacancies are filled in special elections called by the Governor. State budget making is the chief constitutional function of the legislature.

Houses of Unrepresentatives Still *

The membership of California's legislature still does not mirror the state's demographics. For instance, businesspeople predominate, lawyers, while well represented, are declining in numbers. About 75 percent are white, though whites comprise less than 50 percent of the state's population. Fewer blacks (only about 5 % of the Legislature) have been elected in recent years. Latinos and Asians are grossly underrepresented. Only about 30 percent of the legislators are female. None are poor.

Reshaping the Legislature: Redistricting

Every ten years (following the national decennial census) the California legislature is to redraw district boundaries to reflect population changes. The Governor can approve or disapprove. Should the legislature and the Governor fail to agree, the matter goes to the State Supreme Court for resolution.

In 1981, a new and highly partisan reapportionment plan devised by the Democratic majority in the legislature (and signed by the Democratic Governor Jerry Brown, one day before he left office) gave Democrats dominance for a full decade in both the legislature and in California's U.S. House delegation. Though the Democrats still controlled the legislature in 1991, in attempting to redistrict during that year they had to contend with Republican Governor Pete Wilson and a state Supreme Court dominated by Republican appointees. Wilson vetoed the Democratic plans, calling them attempts to

---

*From 1926 to 1965, California had a so called *federal plan*. It provided that representation in California's upper house (Senate) be based on 40 geographic districts, and that no district could have more than one Senate seat. Los Angeles County was most disadvantaged. In 1965, the about 6,820,000 people of Los Angeles County had only one Senator, while the fewer than 15,000 residents of District 28 (Alpine, Inyo, and Mono Counties) also had one Senator. Northern California, which had the majority of counties but not people, controlled the Senate. Finally, after almost 40 years the U.S. Supreme Court rejected the federal plan (effective in 1965). See Jack Carney, *et al*, *Governments of the United States and of California*. (Dubuque, Iowa: Wm. Brown Company, 1965) pp. 223,227.

perpetuate Democratic control, and asking the state high court to draw the new lines. The new districts made no allowance for incumbency or politics and closely reflected population shifts. They signaled massive transfers of political power — to ethnic minorities, most particularly Latinos.

By increasing their majorities in the state Assembly and Senate in 1998, and 2000, and with a Democratic Governor, Democrats were assured of controlling the 2000 census redistricting. But in an uncommon bipartisan collaboration, state legislators attempted to make all districts safely Democratic or safely Republican.

In 2008, the voters approved Proposition 11, giving the power to draw legislative districts to an elected commission. p.62

Reshaping the Legislature: Term Limits Reform

In November, 1990, California voters struck hard at state politicians by enacting Proposition 140, which limited Assembly members to a maximum of six years in office, and State Senators, the Governor, and most other constitutional officers to eight years, counting from 1991.   The vote was clearly against careerist politicians and for a new class of leaders devoted (hopefully) to the true interests of constituents. It resulted in a membership which is much more diverse in race and gender (but not class).

Reshaping the Legislature:
Behavior Modification

Term limits on California state legislators is the towering reform of the present generation of reforms in California. It issued, as had Proposition 112 (in 1990, outlawing honoraria), from public disgust with the legislature in general, and specifically with improper influence of single interest groups over legislators.

Prop. 112 bans honoraria, strictly limits gifts, installs stricter ethical guidelines, and requires legislators to take a class on ethics every year. Members are also barred from voting on matters in which they have a personal financial interest. There are also strict limits on speaking fees. But they are not restricted from earning outside income. The monumental Prop. 140 limits legislator's terms. But these merely put strictures on *individual legislators* yet leave the system itself intact. It seems that not until election campaign spending is effectively limited, and legislative elections are substantially publicly financed, will the views of the voters, not just those of major contributors, be effectively represented.

Assembly Leaders

The *Speaker of the Assembly* is chosen for the post by members of his chamber, and is the most powerful officer in the legislature. Except for the Governor, he or she is probably the most influential official in the state.

The Speaker's important powers as presiding officer include:

1. Appointing the chair, vice-chair, and members of all other Assembly committees (except the Rules Committee);*
2. interpreting the rules and deciding on points of order;
3. recognizing members who wish to speak; and
4. serving as an ex-*officio* member of all committees.

His position as speaker also enables him to raise large sums of campaign money, a role which enhances his speakership.

Other important Assembly officers are the Speaker *pro-tempore,* and the *majority* and *minority floor leaders.* The *Speaker pro tempore* is elected by the Assembly to preside in the absence of the Speaker. The *majority floor leader* is selected by the Speaker, and is his personal representative on the floor. A *minority floor leader,* customarily elected by the caucus of the minority party, leads the opposition party in the Assembly.

Senate Leaders

Like the Vice President on the federal level, the *Lieutenant Governor* presides over the upper house (but usually does not attend). He may not introduce a bill, nor vote except in the event of a tie vote.

The President *pro tempore,* elected to the post by members of the Senate, presides when the Lieutenant Governor is absent, is the most influential Senator, and retains at all times his speaking, voting, and other rights as a Senator. He is also majority floor leader, heads the important Rules Committee (which appoints all committees) and chooses each committee chair, has general responsibility for the administrative functions of the Senate, and oversees the work of the interim committees.

---

* He appoints five of the eight members of the Rules Committee (and its chair).

Figure 1

California Assembly Districts
(2001 Redistricting Plan)

SAN FRANCISCO BAY AREA

KAREN BASS , SPEAKER OF THE ASSEMBLY

LOS ANGELES AREA

Figure 2.
California Senate Districts
(2001 Redistricting Plan)

SAN FRANCISCO BAY AREA

DARREL STEINBERG, SENATE PRESIDENT *PRO TEM*

LOS ANGELES AREA

INTRODUCTION OF BILLS

Only a member of the Legislature may introduce bills. Most *originate* with the Governor, departments and agencies of the executive branch, or pressure groups. A bill is introduced by a member submitting a signed copy to the clerk of the chamber of which he belongs. After being numbered, it is assigned by the Rules Committee to an appropriate committee. About 5,000 bills are introduced in the two-year period.

Consideration by Committees

The crucial stage for most bills is in the standing (or policy) committee. If the bill is important, the committee holds public hearings, welcomes testimony, and may subpoena both witnesses and documents. All sessions are open unless by two-thirds vote the legislature rules a particular session be closed.

A committee may: (1) report the bill out with the recommendation "do pass" (with or without proposing amendments); (2) report it out without recommendation; or (3) table it. About one-half are tabled (or pigeonholed). A majority of the members of a chamber can force a bill out of committee, but this process is seldom used.

THE LEGISLATURE'S NONLEGISLATIVE FUNCTIONS

1. Create administrative departments and agencies, define their activities, appropriate funds for their operation, and frequently to specify their organization and procedures.
2. Participate in amending the California and the U.S. Constitution.
3. Impeach and remove elective state officers and judges, employing procedures similar to those used by Congress on the federal level. (A resolution to impeach must be approved in the Assembly by majority vote. The Senate tries the case, concurrence of two-thirds of its total membership being required for conviction.) An officer found guilty is removed from office. Only one has been convicted in impeachment proceedings.
4. Investigate und. ither single-house or concurrent resolution. Most investigations take place between sessions by committees called interim committees.
5. Consider (by the Senate) appointments proposed by the Governor.

Consideration by the Two Houses

Bills are debated in the order in which they are reported by committees. Debate may be ended by majority vote and the question brought to a vote.

Thus, unlike in the U.S. Senate, there are no minority filibusters in either house of California's legislature. Also, unlike in Congress, the final vote on all bills is by roll call. Furthermore, passage requires (unlike in Congress) a majority vote of the *entire* membership. *

If the second house passes the bill in a form different from the version of the house where it originated, it must be sent back. If the two houses cannot agree on its provisions, a ***conference committee*** composed of three Assemblymen appointed by the Speaker, and three Senators appointed by the Committee on Rules, meets to iron out the differences. If the committee report is not accepted by both houses, a new conference committee is appointed. If after three conference committees on any bill, the houses still disagree, the bill is killed.

Action by the Governor

A bill approved by the two houses and signed by their presiding officers is sent to the Governor. If he signs, it becomes law and goes into effect on January 1 "... next following a 90-day period from the date of enactment of the statute..." except statutes calling elections, or providing tax levies or appropriations for usual state expenditures — which become effective immediately on the Governor's signature.

If the Governor does not sign the bill within twelve days and the legislature is still in session, it becomes law without his signature. The Governor may also veto the bill, returning it to the house where it originated, with a statement of his objections, or he may "item" veto to reduce or eliminate any item in an appropriation bill. The Governor's vetoes may be overridden, but only by a vote of two thirds of the members of each house. **

* Constitutional amendments and bond measures proposed to the people must have a 2/3 majority vote in both houses (2/3 of the total membership, that is). They must receive majority votes of the voters.

**Bond issues and constitutional amendments are not submitted to the Governor.

QUALIFICATIONS, SALARIES, AND PERQUISITES

A legislator must be at least eighteen years old, a citizen and inhabitant of the state three years and for one year prior to the election a resident of the district for which elected.

Senators and Assembly members are paid an annual salary of $116,000, set by an independent Citizens Compensation Commission. They also receive a per day living expense allowance while the Legislature is in session (including weekends), participate in a contributory retirement plan, and receive free gasoline for a leased automobile, and secretarial and telephone allowances.

Members are privileged from arrest, except for treason, felony, or breach of peace, and are not subject to civil process during a session and for fifteen days before and after.

In 2009, their *per diem* living expenses amounted to about $33,000 per year.

SESSIONS

Like Congress, California's Legislature meets in annual general sessions, and in special (or extraordinary) sessions.

From 1946 to 1967, it met in general session only in odd-numbered years and then only for 120 working days. Under the late Democratic Speaker, Jesse Uhruh, the Constitution was amended (1966) to provide for annual general sessions, and the Legislature became a full time professional body. This initiated a nationwide trend.

General sessions begin on Monday after the first day in January and are of indefinite duration. Like Congress, the California Legislature may terminate its annual sessions whenever it chooses.

The Legislature may also be called by the Governor into special session at any time. He lists the subjects to be considered, and may add additional items, and the Legislature may legislate only on subjects he lists. Special sessions are between regular sessions or are concurrent.

WILLIE BROWN JR. Like the illustrious Speaker Jesse Unruh before him, he rose from abysmal poverty in his native Texas to prominence in California as a populist state Assemblyman with a focus on civil rights.

Elected Speaker of the Assembly in 1980, a brilliant strategist and manipulator, Brown held that post longer than any predecessor (14 years). He also became one of the nation's most influential African-American political personages, and after the Governor, the most powerful political figure in California.

But Willie Brown accumulated considerable enmity. This figured prominently in popular support for the term limit Proposition 140.

9 CHAPTER
CALIFORNIA'S JUDICIAL PROCESS

California courts, like federal courts, observe the U.S. Constitution, federal statutes, and treaties even if they conflict with California's Constitution or laws. But they are not subservient to federal courts. They are separate and distinct. And they hear the great preponderance of criminal cases and civil disputes in California, applying statute law, common law, and equity, with as much finality as if there were no federal courts.

The Supreme Court and the Current Political and Fiscal Crisis

Most Americans think, incorrectly, that the Supreme Court is not political. It is. The Court, for instance, intruded into the recent political and fiscal catastrophes by both its action and inaction. *First*, it frustrated the voters' opportunity to vote on a nonpartisan commission to reapportion the legislature. The court mysteriously ruled a proposed initiative to do this (Proposition 26) unconstitutional for containing two subjects. The Court never before dispatched other multiple subjects initiatives from the ballot. There were several.

Second, it ignored the Constitution's framers' attempts to limit borrowing. The Constitution (Article XVI) requires that any borrowing not "...exceed the sum of three hundred thousand dollars ($300,000)..." unless it is for a "single object of work." This means it must be for lasting public improvements, such as for bridges, roads, or schools, *not for the everyday cost of government.* In other words, it forbids borrowing for payment for past operating deficits. The Court failed to enforce the Constitution's limitations on borrowing.

Judicial Policy Making

California's judiciary is possibly the most powerful branch of California's government. The reason is this: in addition to being involved in adjudication, law enforcement, and specialized activities (probate, divorce, suits for damages, etc.), California courts are often dominant in political decision making.

The State Supreme Court interprets the many clauses of California's extremely detailed Constitution, and has the power — which it has not hesitated to employ — to void acts of the legislature and initiatives enacted by the voters which it says conflict with it (or the U.S. Constitution). California courts also interpret California laws and sometimes dictate new meanings to statutes and to the Constitution. And though California legislators shape legislative districts, California courts supervise this function. They also decide if laws are unreasonable or arbitrary, if local officials are complying with the law, or if the Governor is exceeding his powers.

California's Supreme Court has won much praise for excellence and independence, and for leadership of its forceful Chief Justices. Under Phil Gibson, Roger Traynor, and Donald Wright, it often showed the way for the U.S. Supreme Court, and both the Bird and Tobriner Courts were activist. Most of the landmarks of the law during their tenure resulted from judicial activism, which often asserted a doctrine of "independent state grounds" to provide individual rights beyond those mandated under the U.S. Constitution.

But with the liberal-activist majority replaced by more cautious and more conservative Justices now led by Chief Justice George, many see little prospect for much activism, but instead expect the Court to continue to look for guidance to the U.S. Supreme Court, and to defer to the legislature and the Governor.

Though most of the Justices were appointed by rather conservative Republican Governors, California Supreme Court rulings such as the 1996 decisions permitting limited exceptions to the "three-strikes-and-you're-out" law, and decisions making it easier for some battered women to prove they killed in self-defense and win acquittals,* indicate that the Court may not be so easily categorized. Overall, though, they tend to be pro-business and pro-prosecution (in criminal cases).

STRUCTURE OF CALIFORNIA'S JUDICIARY

SUPERIOR COURTS

Superior courts are countywide general trial courts. They consider all felony trials, juvenile criminal cases, domestic relations matters, probate of wills, and civil cases. Very large counties have specialized divisions. Appeals go directly to the Supreme Court if the death penalty is involved, otherwise they go to a court of appeal.

Courts of Appeal

There are six courts of appeal districts (Los Angeles, San Francisco, San Diego, Sacramento, San Jose and Fresno). Three judges sit on a case, and decisions are by majority vote. Juries are not employed since questions of law, and not of fact, are usually involved.

Courts of appeal have no original jurisdiction. They hear only appeals from trial court actions, and decisions of quasi-judicial boards and commissions. Appeal from their decisions is to the Supreme Court (if it accepts the appeal). Most cases get no higher than the court of appeal.

The State Supreme Court

The *State Supreme Court* has a Chief Justice and six Associate Justices. Except for issuing writs, its work consists almost entirely of deciding appeals on questions of law from lower state courts and reviewing orders of the Public Utilities Commission. It generally hears only about five percent of these appeals. The Supreme Court must review all cases entailing the death penalty.

The Court has original jurisdiction to issue writs of prohibition (to keep a lower court from asserting jurisdiction over a case), *mandamus* (to force an officer to act in accord with legal obligations), and *habeas corpus* (a court order directing an official who has an individual in custody to bring his prisoner to court and there demonstrate cause for the detention). Decision is by majority vote, and is final unless there is a possible conflict between state law (or its interpretation) and the U.S. Constitution or federal law. The U.S. Supreme Court, but no lower federal court, reviews its decisions.

How Judges Are Selected*

Trial court judges are elected by district to six-year terms. Elections are generally not hotly contested. Vacancies on the bench in these courts are filled by the Governor.

Courts of appeal judges and Supreme Court Justices are initially appointed by the Governor with the approval of the *Commission on Judicial Appointments*. After appointment, their names go on the ballot for confirmation at the next gubernatorial election, and again for retention upon expiration of the term they are filling. Then after another twelve years in office, the particular judge must face popular election to decide if he or she may continue in office. The ballot contains the incumbent's name, without opponents.

Until 1986, no Supreme Court Justice (or court of appeal judge) failed to receive a majority of "yes" votes. In the 1986 gen-

*To be a judge in any California court, a person must be a practicing attorney in California.

Chief Justice Ronald George

eral election, however, Chief Justice Rose Bird and Justices Cruz Reynoso and Joseph Grodin lost in their re-election bids, thus ending a 30 year liberal domination of the Court. The principal voter complaint was that they (and particularly Bird) were "soft on crime" and specifically were responsible for the Court's failure to order an execution of any death penalty during Rose Bird's tenure. Currently, the Court has a solid conservative majority.

How Judges Are Disciplined and Removed

The Supreme Court may discipline or remove a judge (or a commissioner or a referee) upon recommendation of the *Commission of Judicial Performance.* (This is seldom done.) Any judge found guilty of a felony or a crime involving moral turpitude, such conviction having been upheld by a higher court, *must* be removed by the Supreme Court.

The Supreme Court Justices themselves may be censured, removed, or retired on the basis of a recommendation by the *Commission of Judicial Performance,* approved by a tribunal of court of appeal judges selected by lot.

Judges may also be recalled or impeached.

The Judicial Council

Like most states, California has a *Judicial Council* to overlook the administration of its court system. Comprised of a board presided over by the Chief Justice, it establishes rules of court procedure and administration, advises (and at times decrees) procedural improvements, and recommends statutory and constitutional changes.

CALIFORNIA COMMON LAW, STATUTE LAW, AND EQUITY

Statute law is **legislated law.**

Common law is judge made law, based on the principle of *stare decisis*, meaning that as far as possible a case is decided on the basis of earlier similar cases. Though common law is today largely superseded by state statutes, it remains the foundation for California's legal system.

Equity supplements common law, providing substantial justice where the strict application of common law would result in injustice or hardship. Two examples would be a court order forbidding an action (e.g., a union going on strike) that would cause irreparable damage, or one requiring an act (e.g., that a person fulfill a contract). The typical remedy in statute or common law, on the other hand, is money damages awarded only after the hurt has been done and the injured party can show what he suffered.

THE JUDICIAL COUNCIL

Like most states, California has a *Judicial Council* to overlook the administration of its court system. Comprised of a board presided over by the Chief Justice, it establishes rules of court procedure and administration, advises (and at times decrees) procedural improvements, and recommends statutory and constitutional changes.

CIVIL PROCEDURE

Civil cases involve two or more entities (private persons, businesses, or government agencies) and proceedings to enforce a right, or obtain compensation for its violation. They are distinguished from criminal cases, which involve offenses against the law of the land.

Legal action is started when an entity (the plaintiff) sues another (the defendant), before a judge alone, or by a judge and jury, a full jury of twelve (unless both plaintiff and defendant agree to fewer), a three-fourths vote being needed for a decision. There is no presumption of innocence of the defendant, who can be held liable if there is a determination of a *preponderance of evidence*, that is, a more than 50 percent probability of guilt. The defendant *must* testify if called. The judge may raise or lower damages awarded by the jury. The parties must abide by the court's ruling on the case or risk being held in contempt of court and liable to a fine or jail sentence. Most cases never go to full trial, but are settled out of court because this may be cheaper, more convenient, less aggravating, or quicker.

GRAND JURIES AND TRIAL JURIES

California employs the standard jury system used in the U.S. *Grand juries* of 19 citizens in most counties, nominated by county judges and chosen by lottery, investigate local agencies. They also hand down criminal indictments of suspected felons.* Proceedings are secret, and the accused may not have an attorney present, or cross-examine witnesses.

The *trial (petit)* jury makes a determination of facts, finding the accused guilty or not guilty (by unanimous vote in a criminal case). The judge decides all questions of law. The accused may waive a jury trial.

There are usually 12 citizens on a trial jury, but there may be a lesser number for a misdemeanor trial or a civil case. In a civil case three-fourths of a jury may render a verdict. Names of prospective jurors are taken from DMV records of licensed drivers and from other lists. In 2000, jurors pay was raised from $5 to $15 a day.

* The district attorney usually files an *information* against the accused instead of taking his charges to a grand jury. Only in a relatively few instances when notorious crimes are entailed or, for instance, a public official is involved, does he seek indictment.

FELONIES, MISDEMEANORS, AND INFRACTIONS IN CALIFORNIA LAW

Felonies: Serious crimes (e.g., homicide, arson, certain drug law violations, kidnapping, robbery, forgery, aggravated assault) punishable by imprisonment in a penitentiary for a year or more (or by death). A person accused of a felony is tried by a jury, but may waive it.

Misdemeanors: Less serious violations of law (e.g., driving under the influence, disorderly conduct, petty theft) punishable by a fine or sentence to the county jail (or both). They are usually tried in summary process without jury, though the defendant may plead not guilty and demand a jury trial.

Infractions: Less serious than misdemeanors, they constitute the bulk of the violations defined in the California Motor Vehicle Code. Usually the person cited simply goes to the clerk of the court and pays for the ticket though he (or the prosecutor) may ask for a court trial, where guilt or innocence is decided by the judge (or by a special commissioner in some counties), if the infraction is a traffic offense.

CRIMINAL PROCEDURE

In criminal cases, the government is always the injured party, and thus the one which initiates proceedings. When arrested by a police authority, an accused is "booked" for a named offense. If the booking is for a felony, the district attorney decides whether to file a felony charge. If so charged, the accused goes before a judge of a trial court for a preliminary hearing. If the defendant can not afford an attorney he is supplied a court- appointed attorney. Most felony defendants require court-appointed attorneys.

The judge informs the accused of his legal rights. If the accused pleads guilty, or if the judge feels the evidence warrants, he commits him to the trial court. If an information against the accused is signed by the district attorney, or the county grand jury votes a true bill of indictment, the defendant appears in superior court where he or she enters a plea,* and may opt for a jury trial. The defendant is presumed innocent until proved guilty beyond a reasonable doubt.

The district attorney presents the government's case; the counsel for the accused pleads the defense case; witnesses testify and are cross-examined; ** the defense counsel summarizes his case; and the government's attorney follows with a final argument. The judge then instructs the jury on the law applicable to the case, and the jury — by unanimous vote — must render a verdict based on the judge's instructions and the evidence. If the verdict is guilty, the presiding judge, after receiving a probation report, passes sentence according to the law — a fine, a prison term, or even death. During the interlude, the defendant's attorney may have asked for a new trial or filed for appeal.

With misdemeanors, procedures are generally simpler.

*Most cases are plea bargained, a procedure in which a lesser sentence is arranged in exchange for a guilty plea, and the trial phase is eliminated.

**The defendant does not have to testify. He or she can invoke a Fifth Amendment right against self-incrimination.

10 CHAPTER
Local Decision-Making Institutions

Although local units of state government are not mentioned in the U.S. Constitution, California (like all American states) has created them, and in its Constitution and statutes determines their functions and organization.

THE LOOTING OF LOCAL GOVERNMENT BUDGETS

In recent years, to balance deficit encumbered budgets, the State of California has looted local government budgets. It is not that local governments are flush. They have been badly overstretched for over . 29 years. Proposition 13, in 1978, deprived them of most property tax funds and provided that local tax measures must be approved by a 2/3 vote of local voters.*

Counties have been hardest hit (and thus are more dependent on the state and federal governments). Cities do not have the burden of human service programs as do the counties, have greater flexibility in raising revenue, and enjoy more political clout because their mayors are higher profile than are county officials.

Governor Gray Davis continued the practice of Governors Pete Wilson and George Deukmejian: keeping local governments from full financial independence. His 2003-2004 budget continued

* Since 2000, taxes needed for repairing school facilities bonds require approval by only 55% of the local voters.

Figure 1
California's 58 Counties

Source: California State Controller

the plundering. Local government budgets were reduced by about $825 million. Governor Schwarzenegger supported a constitutional amendment to prevent state looting of their funds. It passed in 2004, (Proposition 1A), amending the Constitution by limiting the state's power to raid local treasuries. However, the state is not fettered in any real emergency.

During the next decade, when hundreds of thousands of state and local government workers retire and begin collecting benefits, it will probably be the biggest issue facing state and local governments. State and local politicians, under pressure from public workers' unions seeking more money, have awarded them unsustainable pension benefits. They awarded pension benefits instead of pay which would be paid on a pay as you go basis. Thus, they could avoid raising taxes and hopefully hide the bill. This means that future generations will have to pay for services they did not receive. When the pension bills come due, politicians will probably try to use the usual backup, a bond issue. But that would be unconstitutional unless approved by a popular vote.

COUNTY GOVERNMENTS

There are three types of local governments in California: county, city and special district.

Counties are administrative subdivisions of the state. California has 58. The most populous (Los Angeles) has about 10 million people, the least populous (Alpine) about 1,220. The largest in area (San Bernardino) covers over 20,000 square miles, the smallest (San Francisco) fewer than 100.

Each county is required to elect a governing body — a board of supervisors, and every county must elect a sheriff, a district attorney, and an assessor. Most counties also have a chief administrative officer (appointed by the board of supervisors), a clerk, a recorder, and a legal counsel.

By far, the greatest county expenditures are for *public assistance and public safety*. The biggest revenue source is state agencies. Counties serve as agents of the state in operating health and welfare programs. But they are also local units of government in providing fire, police, courts, school districts, libraries, and other services. Inevitably, the state's priorities get precedence.

Most California counties (46) are **general-law counties** organized under uniform laws enacted by the state Legislature.

But most large counties are **home rule. A home rule (charter) county** has greater flexibility in determining the number of supervisors, providing for a county-manager system of centralized administration, and combining county offices. Any California county may draft a home-rule charter (which must be approved by a majority of voters voting in a special election).

San Francisco (a charter county) is the only **consolidated city-county** in California. As the City and County of San Francisco it has one legislative arm, one police force, and one set of financial officers.

City Governments

Coming into being at the request of their residents, cities are (unlike counties) more a local unit of self-government than administrative subdivisions. They supply an extensive series of mostly physical services rather than social services. There are nearly 500 of them incorporated in California.

They receive nearly three-fourths of their revenues from city taxes and service charges, and expend more for local public safety than for anything else. They receive about 15 percent of their revenues from state and federal governments.

In California, most large cities are **charter cities.**

Plans of City Government

Under the **strong-mayor plan** of city government, the

mayor is elected by the voters independently of the council, plays a major role in both policy formulation and administration, and has a veto over council ordinances. Los Angeles and San Francisco are among the few California strong-mayor cities.

In a **strong-council plan** of the city government the **council** has primary responsibility and power of both policy-making and administration. The mayor is simply a member of the council selected by it to preside, has mostly ceremonial functions, and no veto power.

In the **council-manager plan**, a popularly elected **council** enacts ordinances, adopts the budget, and appoints the **city-manager**. The manager directs all city departments, and prepares the annual budget. He is responsible to the council and may be removed by it. The mayor presides over the city council and performs ceremonial functions. This plan is more widely used in California than in any other state.

Under the **commission plan** of city governments, popularly elected commissioners serve collectively as a legislative body and individually as heads of departments. There is no separate executive. Since Fresno dropped the form in 1959, in favor of the council-manager plan, no California city has indicated interest.

Special Districts

Special districts are the most varied and numerous of all units of government in California, ranging from large regional districts such as the Metropolitan Water District of Southern

California to local mosquito abatement districts. Their annual financial transactions exceed those of all cities and counties of the state combined.

California uses special districts on a wider scale than does any other state. School districts are the most common. Others (now totaling about 5,000) deal with matters such as water supply, sanitation, fire protection, air pollution control, flood control, irrigation, and highways — problems which are not coterminous with city and county boundaries.

They secure funds by taxing property owners within the district, by charging fees for goods or services, and from state aid.

Regional Governance

In California, nearly all important local powers (e.g., over land use) are retained by local officials. But many of California's most pressing problems, such as growth management (e.g., air quality and water and waste management), and transportation — are increasingly regional in nature. Being regional, they require regional solutions, probably through regional governance.

While there are no regional governments in California, there are a number of voluntary associations of local government agencies to deal with regional problems. Today, most areas of California are within the jurisdictions of regional agencies.*

With the 2008 Recession, local governments have been hard hit. Los Angeles ran a deficit of over $420 million in 2009.

* Examples are the Southern Califorr . Association of Governments (SCAG) and the Association of Bay Area Governments (ABAG).

BIBLIOGRAPHIC NOTE ON CURRENT SOURCES

We have in California a number of worthy reference sources on our state's governments and politics. *The California Political Almanac* is a remarkably comprehensive source book on California's political process, issues, and practitioners. The *California Handbook* is the standard guide to locating sources about California state and local government. *The California Roster* is also highly useful, as are *The Encyclopedia of California*, and *The California Almanac*, *The Almanac of American Politics*, *The California Statistical Abstract*, and *California Cities and Towns.*

California State Publications, issued monthly by the California State Library, Sacramento, is the most extensive list of state documents. The state's library is itself a fertile source, as is the Bancroft Library at the University of California at Berkeley, the California Historical Society's Library in San Francisco, and the Huntington Library in San Marino.

Major newspapers, and particularly the *Sacramento Bee* and the *Los Angeles Times*, feature current information and opinion on California topics. The *California Journal*, published monthly in Sacramento by the California Journal Press, is vital to staying abreast with California issues, politics, and government, and *The California Government and Politics Annual*, also published in Sacramento, is a yearly anthology of *Journal* articles.